EARTH
SIGNS

EARTH SIGNS

GREY WOLF

WITH ANDY BAGGOTT
AND MORNINGSTAR

GRAMERCY BOOKS
NEW YORK

This 2006 edition is published by Gramercy Books, an imprint
of Random House Value Publishing, a division of Random House, Inc., New York,
by arrangement with The Ivy Press Limited.

Gramercy is a registered trademark and the colophon is a trademark of Random House, Inc.

Random House
New York • Toronto • London • Sydney • Auckland
www.randomhouse.com

Art director: Peter Bridgewater
Designer: Sara Nunan
Editorial director: Sophie Collins
Commissioning editor: Viv Croot
Editor: Christopher Westhorp
Picture research: Vanessa Fletcher
Illustrations: Chris Orr Associates
Bead work: Valerie Kieffer

Printed and bound in Singapore

A catalog record for this title is available from the Library of Congress.

ISBN 0-517-22744-4

10 9 8 7 6 5 4 3 2 1

DEDICATION
To my ex-wife for her patience, my sons for their
questions, and especially to Rebecca Patterson, who probably
isn't even aware of the extent of her influence on me.
Grey Wolf

Readers in the southern hemisphere should reverse the meanings and
powers of the North and South Winds throughout (see page 102).

contents

vi

PREFACE

vii

WHERE TO BEGIN

viii

INTRODUCTION

PART ONE

1

THE MEDICINE WHEEL

4

THE POWERS OF THE EAST

9

THE POWERS OF THE SOUTH

12

THE POWERS OF THE WEST

16

THE POWERS OF THE NORTH

21

THE STONE PEOPLE

26

THE PLANT PEOPLE

32

ANIMAL TOTEMS

PART TWO

39

THE FOUR WINDS

44

CYCLES OF THE MOON

52

THE 13 MOONS

102

**THE EARTHWEB
AND THE HEYOKA WHEEL**

106

LAYOUTS FOR THE EARTHWEB

118

PLACING YOUR WATAI

122

THE MOON CHARTS

130

INDEX

132

ACKNOWLEDGMENTS

PREFACE

All living things are one and all are connected to one another on the Earthweb; every plant and creature has lessons that they can teach us. The Earthweb is a medicine wheel, and such wheels can be seen in the traditions of all Earth peoples and all ancient cultures, each expressing it in their own way.

Throughout the whole of creation there have existed opposites—light and dark, day and night, male and female, and so on. We find this duality running through every strand of the Earthweb. Even an atom contains positively and negatively charged parts. Anything that does not contain its opposite within itself is unbalanced. The Earthweb will try to show you the balance between these opposites. A man who has not found the feminine within himself is an unbalanced man. This sort of man uses his power and dominance to drive through any obstacles he encounters without a care for, or recognition of, what the consequences might be. He may be very powerful and successful, but he will never have found the North, the place of wisdom. Likewise, a woman who has not found the man within herself is a victim who is dominated by all. She gives her power away too easily, and this stops her progression on the wheel.

Everything and everyone needs to find this balance if they are to create opportunities for progression. Earth Signs is designed to help you to locate your place on the wheel of life and to find the connections that will enable you to restore the balance and harmony in your life. Earth Signs is not doctrinaire; it is a way of looking at and doing things, but not the only way. You don't have to be a Native American Indian to use this book. You just have to be an Earth person, someone of the Earth who realizes that there is more to this planet that just the physical. Someone who has begun to ask questions and seek answers.

Earth Signs is divided into two parts. The first part provides you with an overview of my understanding of the medicine wheel. The second part gives you the practical information about how to utilize that knowledge to build your own unique spiritual foundation from which to discover more. For those of you who consider yourselves well along your spiritual path, it will give you a new perspective, and as you will know, from new perspectives come new learning. Earth Signs will help you to connect with those lessons so you can discover where you truly belong and what you have within yourself to teach others. The only way you can change the world is by first changing yourself. Then you can show balance through your example and so help others to change. We are all learners and teachers.

WHERE TO BEGIN

Earth Signs is about the Earthweb, a medicine wheel which is both simple and complex; easy to begin to understand yet infinite in its depth and power. Think of the circle and the wheel, shapes of recurrence and regeneration which encompass everything from the atom to Mother Earth. It offers a framework for all of us within which to share the Earth's power, correct our imbalances, and restore individual harmony.

PART ONE

In order to harness and share the power of nature, we must first try to understand it. By looking at the natural world and reading the Earth signs you can learn about your own inner being. The first section puts things in context, explaining the four sacred directions and the nature of the animal, plant, and mineral spirits which exist in the world.

PART TWO

This section describes the strengths, weaknesses, needs, and attractions of people from each of the twelve moons, and explains in detail the moon's cycles and phases, the powers of the sun and moon, and how to create and use your own personal wheel to offer you guidance and invoke assistance.

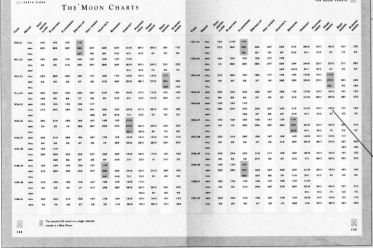

THE MOON CHARTS

To begin working with the wheel we need to know our moon according to the Native American shamanic tradition. By locating our birth date on these charts we can work out which phase of which moon we correspond to.

INTRODUCTION

ABOVE
A typical Plains
Indian hide painting
depicting a battle
between the Lakota
and Blackfeet.

RIGHT
The arrival of
European settler
farmers onto the
Plains meant the
end of a way of life
for the buffalo-
hunting nomadic
tribes. Soon, crops
grew where the
buffalo had roamed
and grazed. The
delicate balance of
man and nature was
upset; plows,
drought, and erosion
combined to create
dustbowls.

In 1897 my great-grandfather decided to become part of a relocation scheme to take Native American Indians from the Pine Ridge reservation to Texas and teach them farming skills. Eighteen families moved, led by my great-grandfather. His son, my grandfather, became what they identified as a Wichasha Wakan, a holy man.

When I was born, my grandfather was asked to name me. He named me Wesley's Skyhorse, Wesley being my father's name and Skyhorse being the messenger in his vision. My grandfather was also asked to give me the names to go on my birth certificate. He chose Grant Edward in honor of Ulysses S. Grant and Robert Edward Lee, the two opposing generals of the American Civil War. He did so because I would spend my life in conflict with myself. I was an Indian, a Lakota, but I would be brought up and educated by the dominant society, Western civilization. This conflict has stayed with me throughout my life; my grandfather taught me one way and my Western education taught me another.

When I was seven, I went to live with my grandfather. He was my friend and not just my teacher, not just my grandfather. I was the only grandchild who would question him: I wanted to know the hows, whys, and whats; I wanted to know about spirit; I wanted to know about the medicine wheel he had shown me when I was five, and I wanted to know how to work with it.

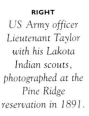
US Army officer Lieutenant Taylor with his Lakota Indian scouts, photographed at the Pine Ridge reservation in 1891.

My grandfather was born during the early years of reservation life. His teachers were those who had fought the "Indian Wars." He knew some of the people who had been at Greasy Grass (Little Big Horn). He knew survivors of Wounded Knee. He had sat at the fires and listened to them talk. He had learned the old ways, and it was these ways he taught me, as he understood them and had seen them change. He taught me to look back, not to find out the way we were, but to find the way forward.

I wanted to know things that my father wouldn't even talk about, so it was my grandfather that I turned to for the answers to my questions. It was my grandfather who led the ceremonies that my father refused to take part in and that my mother denied existed. My grandparents became my parents. They taught and guided me in all matters.

When I was 17, I decided to enlist in the US Marine Corps rather than wait until I was drafted. I spent five years in the marines and the experiences I had in Vietnam caused me to seek isolation when I returned. So upon coming home, I picked up my rifle and fishing rod, bought a small boat, and headed off into the swamp.

My grandmother had died while I was in the military, and I had not been given leave to attend her funeral. During the time in the swamp, much of what my grand-mother had taught me came back to mind. I had thought my grandfather was much more important than she was, and I didn't think that I had learned anything from her. I was wrong. Not long after that, my grandfather died and that left me at a loose end. He had trained me so I could take his place as spiritual leader in my community, but when I looked around, there were only three of my people left. They neither needed me nor wanted me, so I began a period of drifting.

I finally settled down, went to college, then university, and started teaching. Working with emotionally disturbed girls at a wilderness camp, I began to understand just how powerful the teachings that my grandfather had given me were. I taught life skills from my spiritual perspective; about the watai, *about relationships with plants, and about the medicine wheel.*

On later travels I learned from mechanics, farmers, and all sorts of people whom you would not expect to be teachers. Wherever I went, I always ended up teaching, counseling, or advising. I always reverted back to the path of the wolf, the teacher, and I found it easy.

When I moved to England, I realized that my work as an advisor and teacher was my vocation. Since then, I have been a self-employed teacher and advisor, going to businesses, schools, and public gatherings, showing people the connections—the Earth signs—that make up the Earthweb. I think of myself as employed by the Creator to show his children what I have learned and continue to develop in the way of spirit.

Many people ask me what I am; what I do. I am not a medicine man of the Lakota people because I am not following the old ways in their traditional sense. I don't sing or pray in Lakota; I use English because that is the language I was taught and allowed to speak as a child. I use some Lakota terms like mitakuye oyasin, *like* Wakan Tanka *for the Creator, but my path led me a different way. I am a medicine man of Mother Earth. I understand my way and work with that*

ABOVE
A Plains Wichasha Wakan *holds aloft his medicine bundle at sunrise.*

LEFT
Sitting Bull's Lakota name was Tatanka Iyotake. He was a powerful Wichasha Wakan *of the Hunkpapa Lakota and a member of the* heyoka *fraternity—those who had dreamed of thunderbirds. He is pictured here in 1885 wearing a crucifix that had been presented to him at a peace council in 1868.*

way. My way was founded upon the teachings my grandfather gave me, which, in turn, were founded upon the ways of my ancestors, but a great deal of it has now grown into something very different: my own understanding of how things are.

I have done many things in my life, and all these experiences have taught me lessons that I have integrated into my way. The visions and experiences I have had have created my medicine wheel, my way, my understanding.

All my life I have sought visions. Often I get a vision in which I see a buffalo. It appears on a hill right in front of me. It is neither night nor day but somewhere in between. The buffalo may be white, it may be black, or it may be somewhere in between. It is this variance in color that tells me what way my life is heading. The lighter the color is, the more I know that I am doing things correctly. The darker it gets, the more I know that I am heading the wrong way. Throughout my life I have been guided by it.

After my grandfather's death, I tried to avoid what I saw. I tried to fight against being a person of the Earth and tried to be Western, but I was not happy. Many things went wrong in my life. Everything went awry because I was going the wrong way.

It wasn't until I went to England that I realized that I was normal and it was society that was abnormal. I had spent years trying to run away from my destiny because I was taught by society that the medicine ways were uncivilized and abnormal. I now know this to be false. The only path to peace and happiness comes from looking within, from learning where our imbalances lie and bringing these areas back into balance and harmony.

The only way you can change the world is by first changing yourself. Then you can show balance through your example and so help others to change. We are all learners and teachers.

MITAKUYE OYASIN.

BELOW
Bronze horses in Dallas, Texas. The introduction of the horse created the high point of Plains Indian culture.

PART ONE

ABOVE

*Tom Lovell's Listening for the Drums shows
two Plains Indian braves on a starry moonlit
night. The Pawnee were keen observers of the
stars and recorded astrological charts on
animal hides.*

THE MEDICINE WHEEL

he Western approach to life and thinking is very linear. History is recorded in timelines, and history books talk in terms of beginnings and endings: a civilization began at a certain time and ended at another; a war began and ended on set dates. All that you are taught and the ways you are taught to think have straight-line aspects.

But a day cannot be truly measured in a straight line because it traveled through a circle and within that circle were many other circles throughout the whole day. These circles can also be thought of as cycles or wheels. The medicine wheel is a way of thinking. Rather than thinking in straight lines, the medicine wheel teaches us to think in circles.

The medicine wheel is a physical thing. It can be seen, felt, and touched in some of its forms, but it is very hard to grasp its existence in other of its forms. The medicine wheel is life. For those familiar with oriental philosophy, the medicine wheel could be considered to be yin and yang. In fact, if you study the symbols used by most of the different philosophies of the world, you will see reflections of the medicine wheel. One of the oldest existing medicine wheels in the world is Stonehenge in Wiltshire, England.

A LIVING THING

The medicine wheel is also a living thing, and it is within this living aspect that the medicine wheel becomes difficult to perceive. We are in a state of existence in which it is very difficult to see—from wherever we stand in time—the complexities held within it. The medicine wheel is the nucleus of

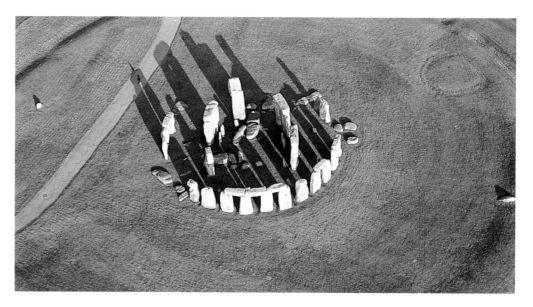

an atom; a form in which very few of us will have seen it. The medicine wheel is also the universe, which no human has seen in its entirety. The universe is the largest physical thing we can perceive, but we are so small within it that we can never see it in its entirety, only glimpse aspects of it. Conversely, the nucleus of an atom is so small compared to ourselves that we cannot see it either.

The medicine wheel is an elusive thing, and because of this elusive nature, since it began being taught, it has had to take on limitations through progressive generations. These limitations were put there to help in the understanding of the whole. When I begin to show you these limitations, when I begin to define the wheel, it is very important that you understand that these definitions are not set in stone. They are not hard and fast, fixed rules. They are only my

perceptions, my way of explaining to you the way in which I perceive the wheel of life.

FINDING YOUR CONNECTION

It is impossible for you to agree with every part of what I show you because you are not me. What I see with my eyes is not the same as you see with your eyes. It is my perspective, and I show it to you

only so that you may see your own perspective more clearly. Using the moon aspects will show you a starting point from which to develop your own wheel.

The medicine wheel can be used to describe the cycle of a day, a year, even a lifetime. It is these three cycles that I will use to explain the workings of the wheel because it is within these three cycles that we can recognize our place on the wheel. The wheel has four directions–East, South, West, and North–but these are not determined by physical aspects. We do use physical aspects to aid our understanding, but, as you will see, to find those things that inhabit a direction, you may have to look a lot farther than in just the physical direction. When we look at each of the four directions, we are looking for connections and signs, and from those we will find our own connection to the Earthweb.

WE ARE ALL RELATED

In the Lakota language, there is a declaration which is "*mitakuye oyasin*," which means "we are all related." We recognize relationships, connections. "We are all related," to many people means that we humans are all brothers and sisters, but to the Native Americans it means much more.

Relationships are to do with dependency and needs, both physical and spiritual. Needs, on a physical level have to do with our physical existence, and on that level I need worms more than I need people. From one perspective, I am more closely related to worms than I am to humans. I do not need humans because humans are not my food. Worms are not my food either, but without the worms aerating the soil, none of the food that I rely on would grow. There is a tendency to rely on our relationships with other humans to fulfill all our needs. The medicine wheel teaches us that we can gain physical, emotional, and spiritual sustenance from all of creation.

THE SEEN AND THE UNSEEN

We are all related to all things, and all things need each other to exist. We are proving this every day when something that has lived on this planet becomes extinct. It needed us to behave in a different way for it to survive. It needed us to do something that we failed to do. Our relationship with it failed. Our medicine with it failed because we did not change our behavior in time to alter our connection and allow it to survive. We destroyed it. That is what Western civilization does to human beings: it destroys our connection. We are talking here about things that we can see and touch, like plants and animals. Earlier we were talking about things that we cannot see like the universe and the nucleus of an atom. So you see there are two worlds, the seen and the unseen. The medicine wheel deals with both worlds and our connection to both those worlds.

ABOVE
It is said that a man's best friend is his dog. The deep and lengthy relationship between man and dog is one of many formed between animal and man in which both parties benefit.

THE POWERS OF THE EAST

*E*ast is the place of beginnings. East is the beginning of the day; the day does not begin at one minute past midnight, it begins at dawn when the sun rises. The East of our lifetime is birth, the time when the child first comes from its mother's womb into the light. The East of the year is springtime; the first day of the year is not January 1, it is the full moon of the equinox, the peak-strength moon of the spring cycle. This is the difference between Western linear thought and the medicine wheel; January 1 is an arbitrary point on the calendar; the beginning of the medicine wheel, however, comes with the birth of the year, that time when new growth begins to spring forth from Mother Earth.

RIGHT
A golden sunrise colors the clouds. Many peoples of the Earth oriented their housing so that the blessing rays of the sun struck their entrances at sunrise; the Navajo hogan and the Plains tipi are two of the best examples.

ABOVE
The eagle is particularly revered by Native Americans, and to the Chippewa the eagle is the spirit keeper of the East, known as Wabun.

THE POWER OF LIGHT

What is the power of the rising of the sun? It is the power of light that enables us to see more clearly. So the East is the place of light. It is the power of clear vision. At birth we come out of the womb and into the light. At springtime the plants send forth their first green shoots to begin their long stretch toward the power of the sun. The power of the East is the power of light. Another way of looking at it is the power of enlightenment.

When I was five, I began asking my grandfather about the medicine

wheel. He took me outside, picked up a handful of stones, and laid them out in a circle. He told me that this was the medicine wheel and began to explain to me the meaning of the East.

ALL THINGS ARE REFLECTED

When we look at the East, we are looking for the light. We can see the source of the light when we look at sunrises, but we cannot always see the benefit of it. Likewise, we cannot always see its destructive nature. Everything has a positive and a negative aspect; everything has two sides. There are two sides to being enlightened. You can become so enlightened that you become cynical; you can become so knowledgeable that the

more you learn, the more you realize how much you don't know! It is part of living by the Earthweb to begin to recognize these things.

This knowledge is probably nothing new to you, but have you really recognized it? Have you given recognition to the East being the time when you were born? Did you recognize that the East of the year, the beginning of the year, was spring and not January 1? Recognition is what working with the medicine wheel is all about, to begin to be able to see and recognize. In doing so you begin to give honor and respect to your connection to the Earthweb.

Now, because we are all related, we put one of our relations in each place on the medicine wheel as an example of the energy, or as the totem of the power of that place. Then we find a color for it, because it will also have a color.

THE POWER OF THE EAGLE

What animal would you say is the epitome of the power of light?

ABOVE
*A warrior raises his shield to the sun and sky
to invoke their medicine. To the Lakota,
Wakan is an all-pervading force, the power
of the universe, and it is manifested in the
blue of the sky.*

Remember what occurs in the East; it is the place where you can see more clearly. I myself find that it is the eagle–a prime example of clear vision. It can be flying a mile up and yet still see a small creature in a hedgerow below it. There are many animals noted for their exceptional eyesight, but when I looked I saw the eagle.

THE COLOR OF THE EAST

So, we now have the East as the place of clear vision, of realization, of beginnings and enlightenment, and the eagle is our power's animal totem. What color is the East? It could be any color–it all depends on you. Each person's perspective is unique to them. You may see many aspects of the wheel the same as I do, but where there are differences that is all they are; there is no right or wrong, only different perceptions. All of these aspects being shown to you are only to help you to understand your wheel because *you* are the center of *your* wheel.

THE POWER OF DEPENDENCY

Now, if the East is about beginnings and the beginning of human life is birth, what power does an infant have? An infant is dependent. In the East everything must be provided from outside. You cannot provide light from your own body, it must come from the sun. Everything in the East is given to you, provided for you, from light to life itself.

BELOW
A Nootka carving of mother and child symbolizes the dependency of the child.

Even the East of the year is the same. A field, if left untended, will yield plants, but it will produce its best crops if it is cared for. Nature produces more if she is given care and her needs are looked after.

This power of the East is very much one of dependency because it requires a lot of care and attention. You seldom come to new realizations or learn something new unless you really strive for it, unless you seek knowledge. The power of the East is a consumptive power because it requires a lot of attention, and the more you pay attention, the more you will learn. Let us now turn through the circle to the South.

ABOVE
This Iroquois painting represents duality. The two figures battling are twin brothers, one representing good and the other evil. The good brother created plants, birds, animals, and man; the evil brother tries to destroy this work. The contest between them leads to a world divided, yet balanced.

ABOVE
*Innocence, curiosity, and trust are
all powers of the child, just as they
are powers of the South.*

THE POWERS OF THE SOUTH

If we move around the circle from the East to the South, we are moving from the sunrise to the noon of the day; from the springtime to the summertime; from the infant to the child. This is a very drastic move when you consider the difference between the infant and the child or between dawn and noon or spring and summer. A lot of changes take place in all three cases.

ABOVE
The Nataska *kachina disciplines children. South-western Native Americans become the kachina spirits in important cycles of ceremonials throughout the year.*

THE POWER OF CURIOSITY

If we look at the South in the same way we looked at the East, what differences do we notice between the two? What are the differences between the infant and the toddler? What are the differences between the powers that they have? Toddlers tend to get into a lot of different things. They cannot be left unattended for a second; for the moment you turn your back on toddlers, they are getting themselves into mischief. Theirs is the power of innocence and curiosity. They have an insatiable curiosity, and do they do things slowly? No! It takes at least three adults to keep up with a toddler. They can be into one thing, lose interest, go over to another thing and totally destroy it before you can cross the room.

If you give a toddler a new toy, the first thing they do with it is taste it. "It doesn't taste good? OK, then shove it in your ear to see if you can hear it! That doesn't work either? Then take it apart and see how it works." The power of the child is furtive curiosity and innocence. "Nothing can hurt me. Mommy or daddy will always fix it. They can fix anything."

MOUSE-THOUGHT

What animal acts that way? For me it is the mouse. I once lived in a lovely little house near London. The only problem was that it was infested with mice. Now mice are a bit like children; they usually come in groups. If you find a mouse, you can be fairly certain that he has at least six of his relatives nearby. I laid down a trap with peanut butter on it. From my experience mice much prefer sticky, sweet peanut butter to cheese; it arouses their curiosity.

I put the trap in the kitchen, out of the way of children's feet

ABOVE
A Northwest Coast animal spirit mask. Native American languages possess no separate word distinguishing humans and animals; both are living things to be identified individually. This reveals much about their attitude to the natural world around them– "we are all related."

George Catlin's depiction of a prairie fire in Missouri. Fire is a sacred spirit, the greatest fire of all being the sun. Naturally occurring Earth fire, such as that from a volcano, is also sacred to Indians.

and went to bed. Now the moment I put the light out and went to bed, all of the mice came out looking for something to eat. They all saw the trap and recognized the smell of the peanut butter, and they probably had a discussion as to who was going to get it. After a short debate, "Uncle Harry" decided he was going to be the one to get it. Well, he went over and began to eat the peanut butter when–bang!–the trap shut and "Uncle Harry" was no more; so the other mice went off and found food elsewhere.

The next morning I got up and cleaned "Uncle Harry" out of the trap and re-set it. That night, the mice came out and one of them thought he was better than "Uncle Harry." He said to himself, "I saw what happened to 'Uncle Harry' last night, but that won't happen to me. I'm better than that. That sort of thing happens to other mice, not to me." Do you recognize this behavior? This type of mouse-thought occurs in humans, too. Incidentally, after that I decided to let nature take care of the problem, and I bought a cat who restored the balance for me.

INNOCENCE AND TRUST

This innocence and curiosity, this "it-will-never-happen-to-me" attitude, is a trait that we all carry throughout our lives. This innocence is the power of the South. The need to learn, to be curious. We always think that things will turn out fine, and they

The inquisitive mouse, furtively curious but perhaps not always careful to learn from mistakes.

ABOVE

A woodland stream in Ontario, the traditional home of the Cree and Ojibwa. Venturing alone deep into the forest can provide the perfect retreat for the vision-seeker.

usually do if we learn to put trust in them. That is another of the powers of the child and of the South: trust. Children actually believe their teachers and trust them to tell the truth. We who have children trust their teachers to educate them correctly. We all have part of this trusting power of the child within us.

THE COLOR OF THE SOUTH

What color is the South? To me, because it is the noon of the day, the hottest part, I see red as the color. Growing up in Texas, we all turned red in the sun. It is the color of fire and of the fire of youth. It is a time of rapid activity. We as humans may wish to rest at this time, but

the remainder of nature is a hive of activity. Noon on a hot summer's day is the most active time in the natural world. The plants are stretching for the sun so hard, to feed from its power, you can almost see them grow. The insect life is at its most active, with butterflies and bees flitting madly from flower to flower. The natural world is at its peak of excitement during the middle of the hot days of summer.

Having gone from birth to childhood, dawn to noon, spring to summer, East to South, we will now travel to the West.

LEFT

A Northwest Coast depiction of a dragonfly. The dragonfly was used by some to symbolize water, the belief being that dragonflies, in their wisdom, always knew where to find it.

THE POWERS OF THE WEST

The West is the time that most readers of this book inhabit; it is the time of the adult. In the year it is the fall, the time when all the plants come to maturity and reach their ultimate phase of development, the end of their growth. If you equate that to a human's life, then you are now supposed to be as the child perceives you. You are supposed to know everything there is to know, to have no more questions that need answering, to feel fulfilled and complete because you have become an adult—but we all know that that is not so.

ABOVE
Albert Bierstadt's California Sunset. The daily miracle of the sunset is a potent image of the power of the West.

When we reach this state of maturity, of adulthood, we finally begin to realize just how little we really know. We become attracted to our own childishness, very set in our innocence—so set, in fact, that it blinds us to the dangers of living. It is a time of fear.

A TIME OF DARKNESS

In the course of a day, the West is the time when the sun sets. The color of the West could be black, blue, or purple, but whatever color

you find there, it will always be dark. In my people's way of looking at things, it is the time when we look within.

The power of the West has this fearsome darkness about it, but you have to remember that all things are reflected. What you see about you is within you. The power of the most evil people on this planet is in your heart. You can be that evil. But, equally, the power of the butterfly, or the rose, or the hummingbird on the wing is within you, too. You can be that beautiful. The West is all about finding out what is within you and learning to balance it so the beauty shines forth.

THE POWER WITHIN

As we grow and develop in our lives, we keep looking in the mirror and we see things about

ABOVE
A mask representing a raven, the bird often identified with the thunderbird.

ourselves that we don't like, that we are ashamed of and don't want other people to know about. We try to escape from them by hiding them all away in a dark "sack." By adulthood, that sack is full, and we spend the rest of our lives dealing with these things. That sack is really within you in that elusive place called the spirit or soul.

THE THUNDERBIRD

The power animal of the West is the one image seen throughout the Native American tribes: on Hopi, Navajo, and Zuni jewelry; in the paintings of the Huron and Iroquois; in the old petroglyphs on the California coast; and even in the artwork of the Inuit–it is the

thunderbird. No one knows of anyone who has seen one, but they all know it exists.

Back in the early days when all the peoples–all the two-leggeds, the four-leggeds, the swimmers, the creepers, and the crawlers, the winged ones–shared their lives in a giving way, all creatures could talk to one another. All lived in harmony giving to others what they needed to live and taking in return only that which was needed for their own survival. But one, the red hawk, could do very little as far as work or assistance was concerned. All it had to give, in exchange for what it needed to live, was its beauty and the marvel of its song.

ABOVE
Sunset over the Smoky Mountains in Tennessee.

ABOVE
A formalized image of the thunderbird incorporated into a Zuni brooch.

THUNDER AND LIGHTNING

For having brought a destructive flood upon the Earth, the Creator called the hawk to itself again, but the hawk was not punished by death, it was not even sent away—well, not far. The hawk was no longer to sing its song and dance its dance to compel the thunder-beings to open the gates. The hawk was to spend its life in service to the thunder-beings.

Now that red hawk does the biddings of the thunder-beings, it listens to their complaints, does their will, and helps them with their job. The flapping of the wings of that red hawk pushes the clouds across the sky from the West, and the sound of those wings is the sound of thunder. Occasionally, the clouds will break, and the bird can look upon the Earth and see where it once lived in great honor. But no longer can it look upon the Earth without doing it harm, for the sight from its eyes is the streak of lightning across the skies.

The red hawk is now the thunderbird. We can never see it because as the clouds break, the lightning blinds us. Anything that is looked upon by the thunderbird is destroyed by the lightning from its eyes. If it looks upon the dry grass, the grass is destroyed. If it looks upon a tree, that tree is split in two. But we must look beyond the fear of the thunder and the destructiveness of the lightning, because with the thunderbird come the rains and the rains are the greatest of gifts: the blood of life.

THE THUNDER-BEINGS

The red hawk spent its life traveling the world, singing its song and displaying its beauty. Out in the high mountains of the West, there was a strange people with an unusual gift: the gift of keeping the gates–for, as we all know, when the rains and the winds come, and the clouds cross the sky in the spring, they come from the West. Each time the rains were needed, these beings, called thunder-beings, would open the gates and allow the clouds to cross the Earth so the rains might fall. The clouds were then called back and the gates were shut until the next time.

The thunder-beings led an isolated existence, and very few people went into the mountains to visit them. After a time, they began to feel dissatisfied and complained to those who did

come, which led to fewer visitors still. They even found complaint with the red hawk, and eventually, it too stopped visiting.

THE CREATOR'S GIFT

The next year the gates were not opened. The rains did not fall; the grasses died; the lakes dried up; and people began to die of thirst and starvation. Those still alive called out for help, and the Creator saw what was happening.

In a situation such as this, the Creator usually intervenes by bestowing upon another being a new gift. A gift that will help solve the problems. So the Creator called the red hawk to itself and gave it a powerful gift, a force that could be wielded for good.

THE POWER OF SONG

The power given to the hawk was that of a song and a dance, performed in a certain way and under certain conditions. The hawk flew to the highest point in the Black Hills and called all the peoples of the Earth to gather.

A lodge was built, and inside it the hawk built a fire and began to dance. The thumping vibrated all the way to the mountains of the thunder-beings. As it danced, the hawk began to sing; and the power of the song was so great that it was heard by the thunder-beings, who were compelled to open the gates. Soon the rains began to fall, and once again, all was well in the world.

THE FLOOD

The same things happened for several years until one year the hawk decided to dance outside for all to see its beauty and for all to hear its real, unmuffled song.

The people were struck dumb in awe and wonder, and the rains came. The hawk stopped, but the rains did not. The rivers overflowed, and the lakes flooded the plains. Many people drowned, and the survivors cried out for help. The Creator looked down and knew immediately what had occurred. Because there was so little time left, the Creator stopped the rains, pushed the clouds back, and closed the gates. The sun shone upon the Earth, and on top of the hill was one bedraggled and sorry-looking hawk. It just stood there with its head hung in shame.

This then is the power of the West. It is full of fear and destruction, but within it is the power of life itself.

THE POWERS OF THE NORTH

I n the cycle of a year, the North is the place of winter. Winter is the time of the hard freezes, of cold, and of rest. Many plants are dormant in the winter, and many creatures sleep through this time—and those that do not tend to reduce their activity; so it is, in the Lakota tradition, the time for looking inward.

The power of the winter is epitomized by a being called Waziya, the white giant of the North, who comes and lays its white blanket across Mother Earth so she can rest and prepare for what is to come when the season turns. The plants have borne their fruit, their leaves have fallen, and they have receded back into Mother Earth.

RIGHT
Yosemite, California, in the winter. Many mountains are significant to peoples of the Earth, and California has many sacred rocks and spiritual sites. The themes of summer and winter occur repeatedly among Native Americans; the Tewa, for example, even consist of Summer People and Winter People.

Waziya is known in the British Isles and America as Jack Frost; and in German folktale, Old Mother Frost shakes her bed, white feathers fly, and then the snow begins to fall. Wherever the ground freezes on Earth, the legends of the land speak of a being who holds the powers of the North and winter.

TIME OF THE NORTH

In the cycle of a day we find that the time of the North is more difficult to locate. It comes sometime between the setting of the sun and its rising the next day. Sometime between the West and the East arrives the North, but the darkness makes it difficult to locate. In the cycle of a lifetime it is equally difficult to locate. It would be easy to say that one goes from infancy to childhood to adulthood and then old age; it is easy to equate the North with the latter years of life, but that is not exactly true.

THE POWER OF WISDOM

The power of the North is wisdom. In many traditions, the

ABOVE
A beautifully carved chest for the storage of belongings. The North is a time of storage, when living things gather together their energy before their new phase begins.

LEFT
The Storyteller *by*
Howard Terpning.
Winter, when people
sheltered for long
periods, was the
ideal time to tell
amusing tales,
recount warrior
exploits, or pass on
knowledge about the
tribal-belief system.

ABOVE
A classic depiction
of Jack Frost by
Arthur Rackham.

elders of the tribe are held in high regard because of their wisdom, but "elders" are not always old in years. What exactly is wisdom?

In the East I talked about the power of enlightenment, of coming into new knowledge, and of the beginning of an idea. Wisdom is the end of that process. This does not mean that the wise person has lost their enlightenment; it means that the person has realized that they need to know more.

Wisdom is very different from knowledge. Earlier I talked about becoming so smart that you become stupid; too much knowledge can be a dangerous thing. Wisdom gives you an insight into how knowledge can be both used and abused, it shows you the balance that needs to be found if knowledge is to be used in a way that is beneficial.

A TIME TO REST

In the cycle of a year, winter is the time of rest. The plants have grown and borne fruit, and now they return to the earth to rest and await the spring. In the cycle of a day, the night is the time when we rest. In the cycle of a life, the North is not just a place of rest in the sense of being in the dark and sleeping. It is much more.

If we look at the old farming ways: in the spring, they planted seeds and tended the soil; in the summer, they were busy making sure the growth continued through weeding, watering, and pest control; in the fall, the harvest was gathered and stored, leaving nothing more to do. When the winter came, the farmers would go into their homes and rest from tending the land.

ABOVE
Indian Hunter in
the Snow *by
Cornelius Krieghoff.
With most life forms
resting, hidden, or
hibernating, finding
food can be difficult
in the winter and
might require an
offering to the
right spirits.*

They would not be idle though, taking this time to do their accounts, to see how much seed was used, and how much fruit that seed had produced, analyzing what crops did well and what crops did not do so well and the reasons why this happened. They would decide what fields to rotate the crops to, which ones to leave fallow, and so on. They would also sharpen the hoes, repair and service the plows, fix the harness, and bag the seeds ready for next spring's planting. Everything would be examined and scrutinized to make sure it was working properly and ready for use.

TIME TO REFLECT

In the course of a lifetime, we go from spring as an infant, to summer as a child, to fall as an adult, and then we keep trying to get back to spring–back to childhood. We keep trying to be young and new all the time. We forget to rest and reflect.

Old age is the time of keeping, the time of remembering. We need to keep the wisdom that lies within knowledge so it can be passed on. This is the time for children to come to the elders and listen to the stories; for the adults to come and seek an understanding of the problems that they are having from the people who have experienced and overcome them in their lives. Sadly, it is not that way anymore. That is just the way it was and should be.

USING WISDOM

We search and look to grow and develop in our lives. We become enlightened when we discover new knowledge, but the finding of wisdom is elusive; it comes sporadically. It is always easy to go out in the day and find something new, but that is not wisdom, it is just knowledge. Wisdom is an understanding of knowledge, of the use of that knowledge, and of the consequences of using that knowledge. It is not just becoming enlightened as to what could be done, but understanding what will be the result of doing it— seeing the potential mistakes before they happen.

The wisdom of knowing what is going to happen to the rainforest if

we don't stop cutting it; of knowing what is going to happen if we don't stop destroying the natural habitats of the barn owl— these bits of wisdom may be small, but the consequences of not heeding them can be enormous.

Wisdom can come at any time that we concentrate and work on something within ourselves and within the circle of our lives on the Earthweb. If you look at the strands, the connections on the web, you begin to glimpse wisdom. It can come to anyone at any time; young people can have wisdom, old people can be idiots. It depends on the individual and what that individual looks at, examines, and finds. Not just what they become enlightened about, but what they actually understand.

GIVING AND KEEPING

Wisdom is the most elusive of the powers; it can come on any day, from any direction and at any time in life. We can only strive for it and try to hold on to it, for it is difficult to retain as well as difficult to find. The North is a time of giving *and* keeping; a time of knowing how much to hold on to and how much to pass on.

The farmers of old harvested the fruits of the fall to sustain them through the winter. If they used it all, they would have nothing to sow the next spring, so they needed to know how much to keep and how much to eat. This, too, is the power of the North: knowing what to release and what to keep safe for later.

THE CYCLE OF LIFE

Winter is also a time of preparation for what is to come. It is both an ending and the dawn of a new beginning. When the light goes out in this world, another light goes on in the unseen spirit world. When in harmony with the universe, everything works in cycles with beginnings, middles, and endings. But for there to be a new beginning, the previous cycle must be brought to completion. Return to the beginning, and you will just run the same old cycle. Step forward into wisdom, bring the enlightenment to its natural conclusion, and you will have the power to be able to step upward and onward on the spiral of the Earthweb.

LEFT
Winter on the Plains—"the time of the cold-maker" – can be very severe. The Mandan earth homes offered greater protection from the bitter winds than the skin lodges of neighboring tribes. Prized ponies often shared the warmth of their owner's home.

ABOVE
*The sound of running water relaxes people
and can soothe the soul. Waterfalls, like
mountains, are spiritual places, and ancient
paintings and engravings can often be found
in their vicinity.*

THE STONE PEOPLE

When I was a boy, I noticed that my grandfather always had a stone in his pocket. It seemed strange to me for an old man always to be carrying a stone with him. The way I got to notice the stone was that whenever my grandfather was saying his prayers, or healing, or counseling, even when he was just deep in thought, out came the stone.

If he was working with someone who had come to him, quite often he would take their hand and get them to hold his stone while he performed his medicine. On one occasion, a man came to him in a lot of pain. He had been working with his horses when he wrenched his shoulder badly. Although not dislocated, it was very badly bruised and he could hardly move it. My grandfather began massaging it. After a while, he took his stone out of his pocket, and rolled it between his own hand and all over the man's neck, down his back, up over his shoulder, and down his arm. When my grandfather had finished, the man raised his arm up and you could tell that the pain was gone.

INYAN AND WATAI

All this fascinated me, and I asked my grandfather about his stone. It was a small piece of agate, nothing spectacular, just rather rounded. He explained to me about *Inyan*, the stone people or rock spirits, who are the oldest beings living upon the Earth. They are actually closer to Mother Earth, in physical form, than any of the rest of her children. *Inyan* hold knowledge and power

RIGHT
Dressed in white deerskin and holding eagle feathers and a rattle, an Apache medicine man incants ceremonial prayers for Mother Earth.

century after century; to them, a decade is like a second of our lives. The knowledge, wisdom, and power that the stone people hold is the strongest of all the peoples.

My grandfather told me that each human being has their own stone or *watai*. Just as all humans have animals who help them, so too *Inyan*, the stone people, form relationships with humans. It is recognized in the name *watai*—a link between the seen and the unseen worlds.

LOOKING FOR A *WATAI*

When you go to look for any stone, whether you are looking for the stones to fit around an Earthweb lunar circle you are building, or the stones to represent the four winds on your web, what you are really looking for is *watai*. Not perhaps as closely linked to you as the one stone that is yours though, because the one stone that is yours is very special. It, like all spirits, like all friends or relationships, is a long-term thing, although not necessarily in close proximity to you at all times. You see, when you find your *watai*, your stone, it will come to you and show itself to you. It will cause you to have to pick it up. It is like a friend calling out when you need to be close.

FINDING MY OLD FRIEND

The first time I went looking for my *watai*, I was about eight years old. I went out alone one summer to do some camping, fishing, and hunting—a freedom we were allowed even at that age because the way of the land and manner in which we were brought up made it reasonably safe for us to do this.

In summertime in eastern Texas, it was reasonably warm and dry, so one needed very little cover or protection at night—just enough to keep mosquitoes at bay. I would tie my canvas between two trees to make a tent and keep it in place with rocks.

As I was walking along, I came to a hill that had been clear cut many years earlier. The topsoil had washed away, and it had very little growing on it, just some scrub and a couple of tough mesquite trees. It was getting close to the time to set up camp, so I decided to camp on top of this hill. It was

RIGHT
A warrior supplicating before the sun. Among the Lakota, inyan *(rock) is one of the four principal forms of* wakan *alongside* wi *(the sun),* maka *(earth), and* skan *(energy).*

clear and it didn't need a lot of tidying, so it seemed like a good spot to set down for the night.

I went down to the woods, cut a few poles, and took them to the top of the hill. I spread my canvas, securing its corners with rocks, gathered some firewood, and built a fire. After eating and watching the sun set, I went inside my tent and fell asleep for the night.

A SHINE ON THE GROUND

During the night I woke up, left my tent and walked a few steps away from it to relieve myself. It was a really dark night because it was the night of a new moon; so the only lights in the sky were the stars and they don't show you much on the earth. Not too far from me, something on the ground was shining. It was shining almost as brightly as the stars in the sky, and it struck me as very strange.

I finished doing what I was doing and walked around a bit. As I walked around, it seemed that as I glanced in the direction where I had seen the shining, something would twinkle at me. It twinkled like a star showing glimpses of an iridescent rainbow: a little blue, a little red, a little white. My curiosity was aroused, and I decided to go over and find out what it was, but the closer I got to it, the less I was able to see it because the light didn't seem to show so well. I took a few steps back and relocated it. As I stepped toward it, the same thing happened—it just disappeared, it

ABOVE

A Pueblo Indian healer. The Pueblos are very rich culturally and have a highly developed system of animal fetishes. Made of minerals and semi-precious stones, many talismans are carved with different animals with potent sacred power. The Zuni believe that as their ancestors emerged, many of the dangerous predators were turned into stone to save the people; their hearts and spirits, however, live on in the stone.

stopped twinkling. The closer I got, the darker it got, and I found I couldn't see a thing. No matter how hard I tried, I couldn't find it, and eventually I gave up and returned to my tent to sleep.

I awoke just as it was becoming light, before the sun rose. I got out of my tent and stood watching the stars get dimmer and dimmer. I stood facing the East, waiting for the sun to rise. I watched the stars fade and the brightness grow until there was just one star left in the sky–the morning star. The sun would rise soon. As the morning star began to grow faint, something shone in my eyes almost like somebody had flashed a mirror. I looked around and could see no one. I didn't see the flash again, but there, in the same direction as I had seen it the night

before, there was something lying on the ground. It was glowing and sparkling. This time it was daylight, the sun had just poked its head over the horizon and I could see clearly what it was. As the sun was rising, its light was reflecting off this piece of what I now realized was stone. I went over and picked it up.

MY *INYAN*

Now it was probably the dullest, drabbest-looking stone I had found or could find anywhere on that hill. It was iron-gray in color, but it had a white streak that ran all around it, like a fault line.

It felt warm in my hand, but the night had just finished, so there was no way it should have felt that warm. Whenever you pick up a stone, unless it has been heated for several hours by the sun, it is cold to touch. This stone, this *inyan*, this piece of rock, was warm.

I just held on to it for a while and thought. I watched the sun rising higher in the sky, and for

LEFT

A decorated war shirt with a beaded bear paw derived from a dream.

some reason I just gave thanks. It was not really clear at that time who I was thanking or what I was thanking, but I just gave thanks. I put the stone in my pocket, packed my things up, and off I went to finish my trip.

A CONNECTION

Now that stone, that *watai*, that brother, stayed with me for five or six years. I used it in ceremonies, and I carried it everywhere with me. It would do strange things: the closer I got to a danger, the hotter it would get. By paying attention to the heat of that rock, there

were several times in my life that I avoided getting into a scrape.

That is the way of *watai*. You never know what they are going to do or just how they are going to do it, but you can be assured that they will do what they need to do to help you on your path.

It is not a matter of having to go out and walk in the woods or go to a stream to find your *watai*—some tales say it must come from the bed of a stream. That is nonsense; *watai* comes when it comes and where it comes. It is not anything other than a connection, no more, no less.

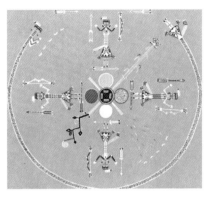

ABOVE
A sand painting of the Arrow People who are made of, and live at, mountains of precious stones.

LEFT
Cheyenne Vision Seekers *by Howard Terpning. Rather than an individual seeking his personal spirit guide, this is a group of men. They are painted in holy whitewash and have lit the sacred pipe, seeking a sign to show them the way out of a crisis facing their people.*

THE PLANT PEOPLE

M y grandfather worked with the land. He and I tilled the soil, rotated the crops, planted the seeds, and reaped the harvest. We farmed in the conventional sense. We grew what we needed to eat, but we also grew a bit more to sell. That bit more was our livelihood, and we lived well from it.

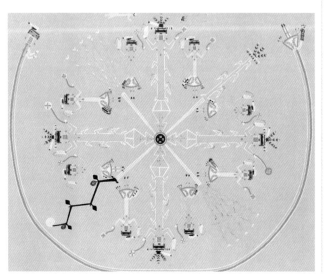

He didn't teach me about the plants, though; he taught me about the planting and the harvesting. He didn't teach me about the trees; he taught me about which were good for building or bow-making. He didn't have the time to teach me about the living spirit of the plants; he worked with them, but he didn't have time to teach me that. My grandmother taught me about the plant people.

My grandmother knew everything that grew on our land. What was planted by men and what just came of its own accord. We had 165 acres under the plow, we had a wood lot, and much more. There were many varieties of plant, and my grandmother knew the names of each of them. She also knew at what time of the year they would be ready to give whatever they had to give and when they needed to be attended to. She worked with the plants and she worked with the trees.

FOR FOOD AND SPIRIT

It was she who taught me the way to blend the *kinnick-kinnick*, the sacred ceremonial smoking mixture used in medicine pipes. She taught me about the use of smoke from burning sage and sweetgrass. Nearly every society uses smoke for a purpose. Frankincense and myrrh were two of the gifts given by the Magi to Christ; two substances to burn, of equal value to the third gift

ABOVE
Wild chicory has nutritional and healing properties. As an herb, it is a diuretic and strengthens the liver.

ABOVE

*A Kutenai Indian woman gathering rushes
from her dugout canoe, photographed by
Edward Curtis. Such crops have many uses
and are harvested with great care and respect.*

of gold. But gold is of value in the physical; plants are of spiritual value.

My grandmother knew which plants to grow and harvest, not only for food, but for spirit. Dealing with the spirit is very powerful because it unites the seen and the unseen worlds. When we take an infusion, like mint tea to help with a fever, we are not only dealing with the physical fever, we are dealing with the spirit cause or effect of that fever. The pleasure of breathing in that aroma affects the spirit and also helps with the healing.

RESPECT

My grandmother taught me how to respect the plants. To do simple things like thank them for what they give. The celebration Thanksgiving originated in a feast given by the pilgrims as a token of thanks to the Indians for having helped them to live. It has now developed into "We must thank God for everything." I agree, but shouldn't we thank the plant as well? To me, that is the most important thing because it keeps our connection, it strengthens that strand on the web.

We need to understand that things don't just come from the Creator; they come from themselves. They come when and where they are needed to help bring balance to the web. Sometimes you have to go and seek them, gather them, not just sit and wait for them to come to you. These are the things my grandmother taught me about, this going out and getting what you need, and how to recognize and harvest those plants that could help you on your path.

THE POWER TO HEAL

The time that all this really came home to me was that time I spoke about earlier when I came home from the marines. I went off into the swamp, and I did a lot of looking at myself and what I was about. Life was not difficult. The weather was hot and the fishing easy, but I got sick. I could not understand the reason why I was

BELOW

A Hopi ceremonial called Soyál, during which the kachina Mana carries the seed corn for sanctification to increase the yield; the village is ritually cleansed of misfortune; and the sun is turned back from its southern course so that it comes again to the Hopi people.

LEFT

Spearmint offers medicinal properties and is one of hundreds of herbs used by peoples of the Earth to effect cures. Such plants are considered gifts from the gods. The Cherokee had a very detailed knowledge, and a typical medicine man was familiar with some 400 species.

ill, and I had no medications with me. It was then that I started to remember what my grandmother had taught me.

I had a fever, so I began boiling my water and drinking mint teas, but I didn't seem to be getting any better. Then I remembered a plant that my grandmother used to collect. She would dry the leaves and crumble them into hot water to make a tea. She would give us this tea to help to bring out a fever. I found the plant and boiled it up into a tea.

It made my gut wrench, and I thought I was going to die. After I had spent several hours cleaning my system out, I remembered that my grandmother never gave it to

ABOVE

Plants and trees must be treated with respect, for they can help heal and nourish the spirit as well as the physical body.

me fresh, she always dried it. After chastising my own stupidity, I built a lattice-work of twigs and dried some leaves over a fire. When I had finished that, I crumbled them up and put them into a tea, drank it, and went to bed.

Four hours later I woke up, sweating like a pig! Everything was wet, but it wasn't raining. By the next morning my fever was gone, I felt good, my stomach wasn't upset anymore, and all I had was a bad taste in my mouth. I think the bad taste was from drinking the fresh leaf tea. I learned a powerful lesson that day about having respect for the healing power of plants.

THE POWER TO HARM

Anything that exists with a power to heal has an equal and opposite power to harm. The old Native American healers knew this and knew that it was only by attuning to the energy of a plant that one can learn how to extract its medicine. My grandmother had this ability, and it is one that I continually strive to perfect within myself.

ATTUNING TO THE ENERGY

When I first went to England, I came across a tree that I did not recognize. It was a yew tree, and I knew nothing of its medicine. There were a few branches lying on the ground, that I picked up and took home. I dried them, stripped the bark, and began carving them.

BELOW
The Crow Mother kachina wears crow wings on her mask and carries a basket of bean sprouts to symbolize the miracle of germination in the middle of winter.

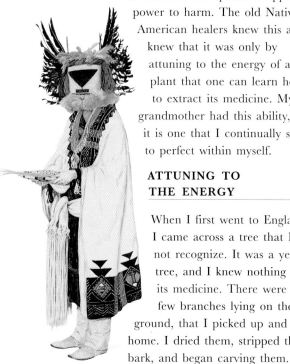

ABOVE
A Hopi girl clutching a plant. During the new moon of February, the eight-day Bean Dance, or Powamu, is celebrated by the Hopi in honor of germination and growth. Every fourth year, all the six- to ten-year-old children learn for the first time from Crow Mother that the dancers are men and not spirits.

As I was working with them, I got a sense of strength, a sense of community and of protection. I read later about the history of the yew tree and discovered that its wood was used to make bows and that at one time it was law that every English adult male had to own a bow and practice with it for the protection of the community.

I had felt all those things before I discovered them in books. I had attuned to the energy of the tree. That is what needs to be done if you are to learn from the plant people. You can read about their energies and what is known about them, but to learn their wisdom you have to feel it for yourself. Everyone can sense these things if they allow themselves to. There is nothing magical or strange about it, it is just an ability that we have forgotten about.

Your relationship with the plants and trees must be a personal one—not just the way of someone else, or what it says in some book. It is through the forming of these relationships that you gain your connections on the Earthweb. It requires you to let go of your ego and your preconceptions; to open your heart and your mind and to allow whatever is needed to come in. This is the only safe way I know to work with the plant people. There are those who try to learn through drinking herbal teas. In some instances this can help, but when the plant is poisonous (like the yew), you have to find another way to access its wisdom. The simplest way is just to ask and wait and see what answer comes back; to make contact with the plant and let its wisdom trickle into your subconscious and finally through to your conscious mind. This will take time and patience, but the reward will make it well worthwhile.

ABOVE
*A representation
of the spirit of
the grass.*

BELOW
*A Navajo
grandmother
weaving wool with
her grandson, an art
taught to them by
Spider Woman.*

ANIMAL TOTEMS

Throughout all the writings of the many peoples of the Earth who have lived in the old ways, their connection to animals is always evident—there was even an English king called Richard the Lionhearted. We learn about our kinship to animals in many different ways, watching and observing them. I have been told that the Cherokee hold the bear in great esteem and honor. They tell a story about it that says that back in the time before everything was formed, there were seven kindred spirits that had to choose what to become. Six of them chose to become human and they became the Cherokee; the seventh chose to become the bear instead. This is why the Cherokee always give honor to the bear as their brother.

THE BEAR

Throughout history the bear has been a significant creature. We learn ways of life from the bear; it revealed the potato to us when we watched it dig it up from the ground and eat it. Whatever a bear will eat is good for a human as well. It may not be socially acceptable to eat the bugs that bears find under trees, but they would not do you any harm. When a bear goes looking for fish, he doesn't look for the perch, he looks for the salmon and the trout—the best. When he goes looking for the berries, the ones he chooses to eat are all good for us humans. If you watch and follow a bear, you can gain much knowledge.

When you observe a bear, you can find very human characteristics in their activities. A bear with a stomachache acts just like a human does: it sits, wraps its arm around its stomach, gently rocking and groaning to itself. It gets flatulence the same as humans do, but bears don't go off to the pharmacist, they go to Mother Earth. They go out and dig up a particular root to eat, which scientists have found contains active ingredients to alleviate stomachache.

When the bear has a headache, it sits and rubs its head like a human. It finds a red willow tree and scratches at its bark. It pulls away the inner bark and eats it. Someone, at some time, saw the bear do this and noticed that shortly afterward the bear was acting like it had no headache at all. They took some of the inner

ABOVE
The Cherokee believe that the water spider brought fire to mankind. This circle represents the world and the sun, and the cross the four cardinal directions and the sacred fire.

ABOVE
Brown bears catching fish as they head upriver to spawn. Learning from the bear, native fishermen have created over-hanging platforms in identical places because of the ease with which fish can be obtained.

bark to a scientist who discovered it contained a natural painkiller, which is now the active ingredient in aspirin.

ANIMAL BEHAVIOR

There are many lessons to be learned from animals by watching the way they behave and finding ways to equate their behavior to our aspirations. What person wouldn't like to fly as high as the eagle? What human wouldn't like to be the predator, only bothering to hunt when they are hungry and relaxing and enjoying their life the rest of the time; never overly concerned by other animals preying on them?

We see animal behavior many times on a physical level without having a comprehension of what

RIGHT
A depiction of the mighty thunderbird.

we are actually seeing or of how we are learning. When I give dreamcatcher workshops, I talk about the lessons of the spider. Dreamcatchers have become popular and originate from Native America, although similar objects have been found in China, among the Aborigines of Australia, and in Africa and South America. The story of the dreamcatcher has to do with the web of living—the Earthweb.

Some time ago there was a Lakota woman who was having a great deal of difficulty with her health. Not that she was really sick with an illness, she was just constantly weary. Her resistance was lower than most, so whenever there were bugs or viruses going around she would get ill. The reason for her condition was her dreams. She had very active and busy dreams that were not allowing her to rest when she slept. We have all had those occasions when we have slept eight, nine, ten, or even 12 hours and have awoken feeling like we have slept just a few minutes. Through the night you would have had many dreams that did not allow you to rest; so in the morning you were more tired than when you went to bed. Well, for this woman, every morning felt like that.

After a while, she went to a *Wichasha Wakan*, a holy person, to seek advice. Together they prayed about

ABOVE
A Crow warrior's amulet, a talon of the sacred eagle. The bird used this to strike at its prey, thus for its owner it was a mighty talisman offering success against his enemies in battle.

the problem and during their prayers the spirit of the spider appeared to them. It taught them how to weave the web of the dreamcatcher and told them that they should weave the web, decorate it, and place something within the web to honor the spider. Then the woman was told to hang it in the place where she slept. The spider told her that all of the dreams that came to her would now have to pass through the web before they would come to her and that the web would filter out the unnecessary and disruptive dreams.

That night the woman hung the dreamcatcher up and placed something within the web to honor the spider as it had instructed her. Then she went to sleep. Just as she had been told, all the dreams went to pass through the web. The dreams that she needed came through and reached her in her sleep. There were still some bad dreams, some good dreams, and some active dreams, but only the dreams from which she needed to learn lessons in order to live her life came to her that night. You see, we believe that dreams and visions are one and the same; they are lessons for the spirit of those that have them.

From that time on, the woman only had the dreams she needed. The spirit of the spider within that web consumed all the unnecessary dreams. Thus she was able to get enough rest, and consequently she regained her health.

Personally, I learned one of my lessons about connections to animals as a child, when I mounted

and rode a mule five miles to the store and back without knowing the adults had been trying to ride that mule at the county fair rodeo for more than seven years. There was a $100 prize for anyone who could sit on his back for eight seconds–and nobody had ever won it. That's how it is with animals. There are those that will work with you and those that will not. Sometimes they accept you because of your ignorance and need and do things for you that they will not do for others. Sometimes it's because you understand them and try to work with them. Learning how to work with any animal is about forming a relationship with that animal, and it is up to each individual to form those relationships.

THE LESSONS OF THE SPIDER

Everyone has animal helpers, both in the physical sense and the spiritual sense, that are there to teach them and help them on their path. Sometimes they just help with everyday tasks; at other times they bring gifts, like the eagle in the East that gives the man or the woman who seeks it an example of a way to be more enlightened.

The life of a creature gives us many lessons. Let us consider the spider. There are a great many people who don't like spiders, and a good few who are frightened by them. If you look at the life of a spider, though, you can learn many lessons about bravery, tenacity, beauty, and much more.

A spider will build its nest high up among the rafters of a cathedral, 30, 40, or 50 feet above the ground. It will attach a strand to the rafter that is so fine it can hardly be seen by the human eye. Then it will launch itself into thin air, trusting in that fine thread to support it until it reaches a place of safety where it can attach the other end of the strand. Thus it will start the weaving of the web. That is brave.

The spider teaches tenacity as well. Tenacity is a nice word for stubbornness. At springtime many people clean their houses and clear all the cobwebs out. They go to bed that night in their nice, clean, cobweb-free house, and they get up in the morning to find new webs have been built to replace the old ones. The only way to stop a spider from living where it wants to and doing what it does is to kill it. That is the power of tenacity. The stubbornness to carry on doing

BELOW
Kestrels, like all birds of prey, were greatly admired for their hunting prowess. Their feathers invoked the power for the wearer.

DJUN'S MAGIC IN THE HOVSE OF THE CHIEF.

ABOVE

The Tlingit have a story about Djun, a female shaman, who had birds as her animal helpers. The birds frightened the spirits that were stopping the tribe's plants from growing.

art. In the Lakota language, there is no word for "art" because art is something that you do as a separate thing in your life in Western civilization. People are artists, and they paint, sculpt, or whatever else they do and call it art. What we Earth people do is make the things that we need for living our lives. Everything that we make has a purpose and is made as beautifully as possible because that is the way it needs to be.

It is like the dreamcatchers. They are a beautiful decoration to hang on the wall, but they are a thing of power, too. The fan that we use to swirl the smoke of the smudge pot around in our ceremonies is not just a feather, it is a highly decorated fan. It is beaded, leathered, and fringed as beautifully as we can make it to give honor to the bird that provided the feathers and to the spirits that we call upon to help us.

The spider does this, too. The spider's web is its home. Have you ever seen a really ugly spider's web? No! They are a thing of beauty to behold, an intricate weaving of beautiful designs. But the web is also a practical thing; it has its purposes. It is not only a home, but also a trap, a net. It is a tool, but a very beautiful tool–as beautiful as the spider can make it.

Another lesson the spider can teach is patience. Patience is one of the spider's strongest suits. The job of the spider is not to weave a web and then go out with a club to catch a fly for dinner. The job

what you want or need to do despite all the obstacles you encounter, all the setbacks you suffer. You can clear a hundred, even a thousand, webs away, but all the time that spider lives, it will build new ones.

The spider understands beauty in the same way that the people of the Earth do. The people of the Earth–that is, those that live in the old ways–have an understanding of beauty that is far more pronounced than the understanding of people who like

of the spider is to weave the web and then wait and wait . . . and wait. It waits until it can feel the web vibrating as the fly that has become caught in it tries to escape. Then and only then can it have dinner.

Most of the spiders that weave webs are female. This gives us another lesson to learn about patience: it comes easier to women than men. The female spider will sit on her web for hours, waiting. Then one day a male spider will come along wanting to do what male spiders do. She may be very hungry, but knows that it is vital for her species' survival that she waits just a little longer. So she allows the male to do to her what he wills, but when he is through, if he is not quick enough, he will become dinner. Patience only lasts so long, and after it can come terrible retribution. Those men who leave their wives waiting at home while they go out would be wise to learn from the spider!

REFLECTIONS

One small, insignificant creature like the spider has so many interesting lessons to teach us "highly evolved" humans.

This is how relationships with animals are found. They are found not just in the vision quest, not just in the spirit of things, but in the physical, too. All things in spirit are reflected in the physical and vice versa.

If you look at an animal and discover something about it that is a reflection of yourself, then it is an animal that has to do with you. If you find in that animal a reflection of something that you need, then that animal is for you. It is a power that you should call upon for help.

PART TWO

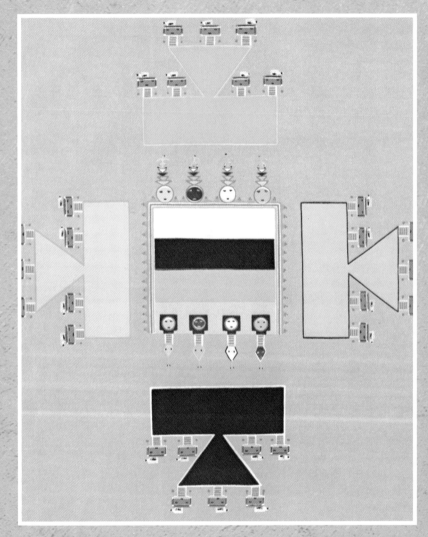

ABOVE

A healing chant sandpainting showing Sun's House (center), with representations for each of the four sacred directions.

THE FOUR WINDS

The Earthweb is built around Toshila, Grandfather Sun, and Inyan, Grandmother Moon: the two powers of male and female, creator and grower. The sun's rotation is fixed in relation to the Earth, whereas the moon's is not. Grandfather Sun is warm, strong, and helpful; Grandmother Moon is fluid, influencing the flow and the waters of life. Together they are like the energies of the male and female.

GRANDFATHER SUN AND GRANDMOTHER MOON

There are four relatively fixed points of North, South, East, and West, also called the four winds, which are marked by the sun's position in relation to the Earth on the solstices and equinoxes and are almost unchanging. The four "days of the sun" fall between the twentieth and twenty-second of March, June, September, and December, and fluctuate slightly due to our global measuring of time using the Roman calendar.

I hold ceremonies on the days of the solstices and equinoxes, because these are the days when the winds are at their most potent. I give my prayers to the four directions to say thank you and remain connected.

THE EAST WIND

Springtime is the place of birth and new beginnings, and stands in the direction of the East Wind. East is the direction of spirit and is represented by the eagle, the totem for the East Wind.

I use the East Wind whenever I want to begin something new or bring something into being. It is most powerful during the spring months of February 11 to May 10. Its most potent day during this phase is the Spring Equinox, after which the influence of the East Wind will begin to wane as it makes its way toward the next part of the annual cycle.

Springtime is the best time to start new projects. It may mean that you have to wait until the cycle arrives at the strongest date to get the assistance that you need. If so, use the time to prepare yourself for a new beginning; it will bring greater power to your prayers and intentions.

Spring is the time of the infant. If you were born on the day of the Spring Equinox, you will be most

ABOVE

A mask representing the sun. As with all the four winds, it is advisable to perform your ceremony upon the actual day of Grandfather Sun, because these are the days of his greatest power.

potent in the early stages of your development, and will have a sense and power of new beginnings. You will have the gift of knowing how to start something new, and this will be a continuing influence throughout your life. For example, as spring-beings move south into the time of the child, they will continue to have the ability to create new beginnings, but will now be learning how to expand upon them. From the South, the spring-being moves to the West to adulthood. Being the opposite to the East, this will be the direction where spring-people potentially encounter the most difficulties, because each new beginning seeks completion, and they may find it difficult to finish what they have started.

Spring-people, therefore, are most compatible with fall-people. They can balance and complement each other during the cycles of creation and completion.

Dawn is the time of the East Wind, and ceremonies held close to the dawning will hold the most power for people wanting to start something new. Amber is the stone that I use to represent the powers of the East Wind, the wind of Grandfather Sun.

THE SOUTH WIND

Summer is the time of rapid growth and expansion, a time to build and consolidate, and is the direction of the South Wind. The energy of Grandfather Sun is most powerful in the South because the Summer Solstice is the day with the longest light during the year's cycle; it is the most powerful day for calling upon the South Wind, after which he wanes to allow for the rising of the West Wind.

In summer or winter, at the times of the North and South Winds, we enter the time of opposites. The time when either

BELOW
The mountains of the Sawtooth range, Idaho, provide the backdrop for the spring flowers that have emerged from their winter rest.

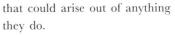

Grandfather Sun is in full power during the summer months, or Grandmother Moon is at her greatest strength throughout the winter months.

The South Wind is represented by the humble mouse and is in full strength during the period of May 11 to August 10, with his day of fullest power on the solstice.

I face the direction of the South Wind to call upon his help for building and growth, or when I am seeking ways of learning how to expand things in my life.

South is the time of the child and summer-people will be most potent during childhood. If you were born on the Summer Solstice, you will have the greatest ability of us all to expand upon new beginnings, and will know instinctively how to make things increase and grow. You will be active and busy throughout your life cycle. As the summer-beings move around the wheel, they will take the gifts of expansion and building into the West and the North. The direction of North will hold the most learning for summer-people who must discover how to rest, how to be quiet and how to keep a balance between activity and stillness. They must also strive to become more aware of the dangers that their innocence tends to prevent them from seeing. Not just the danger of hurting or injuring themselves, but the harm that their actions might inflict on others. The person whose strength lies with the South Wind will have difficulty in seeing the dark side

that could arise out of anything they do.

Summer-people are most compatible with winter-people, because their opposing energies can teach each other when to be active and when to be still.

Midday is the time of the South Wind, a time when everything is flowing and full of life. The stone that I use for this time is the garnet; the fiery red of the heat of the midday sun.

THE WEST WIND

Fall is the time of harvesting and giving; it is the direction of the

ABOVE

Amber (top) and garnet (above), the stones for East and South Winds respectively. The passionate and intense nature of people of the South can be soothed by the calming influence of garnet; this stone is linked to creative thinking and can also bring about a willingness to be part of a team.

BELOW

An eagle-feather headdress. Eagle is the totem for the East Wind. Its clear sight and perception call humans to look to the East, to the place of the rising sun, and to allow enlightenment to rise within. Eagle calls us to aspire to spiritual understanding.

West Wind. The thunderbird is its totem and is at its most powerful during the fall months of August 11 to November 10. Its day of peak strength is the Fall Equinox.

The equinoxes—or the directions of East and West on the Earthweb —are times of balance and equality, when the days and nights are of more or less equal length. Dusk is the time of the West Wind. The stone I use to represent it at the moment is snowflake obsidian. The "snowflake" is an imperfection in the way that it is made; its effect is like the light within the dark. There is light in the darkness of the West Wind, so when the thunderbird comes, and no matter how dark the storm is, there is always good that comes out of it—there is always light in the darkness. This is why I have chosen

snowflake obsidian to represent the powers of the thunder-beings: to remind me to overcome my fears, and to trust that the powers know and will guide me in the right way.

I face and call upon the West Wind whenever I am wanting to harvest the fruits of my labors, or am wishing to learn how to give my gifts to others.

West is the direction of the adult. If you were born on the Fall Equinox, you will have the ability to give and will know how to profit from your efforts. You will also know how to complete tasks. People of the West will be most powerful during their adult years.

THE NORTH WIND

Winter is the time of holding and keeping and is the direction of the North Wind. The white giant Waziya is the totem, holding influence from November 11 to

ABOVE

A Mimbres-style pottery bowl painted with the guardians of the four directions. Such bowls were ceremonially "killed" at their owner's burial by puncturing the base to release the bowl's spirit into the next world.

February 10, with greatest power on the solstice.

I face the North Wind whenever I am wanting to call the qualities of quietness, understanding, wisdom, and knowing into my life. The Winter Solstice is an appropriate time to call upon the wisdom of the elders to help you come to greater understandings. This is the night when Grandmother Moon is at the peak of her power, while Grandfather Sun is at his weakest. The energies of the Earth are resting and rejuvenating in preparation for the new beginnings that springtime will bring.

North is the time of the elders, of the wisdom keepers. Those born on the Winter Solstice will have the ability to hold wisdom and knowledge, and will be capable of deep understanding. The North-people should not hold onto knowledge or experience without allowing anything new to come into being—they will become stagnant and lose what they know.

The time of the North Wind in a night is difficult, if not impossible, to pinpoint, but it is some time around midnight, between sunset and sunrise— between the harvest of the West Wind and the birthing of the East.

The North Wind totem is milky quartz, a very female stone carrying within it the color of the milk that feeds us when we are young. It stimulates our consciousness and truly reflects this time of year—the time of wisdom, or of educated thought.

GIFTS AND LESSONS OF THE FOUR WINDS

Sometimes, the gifts and lessons of the four winds don't seem to show themselves in the individual. This is normally due to the influences in life while growing up; the link between spirit and the mind is easily severed. Mind, as the interpreter of spirit, will disconnect from its spiritual source when influenced negatively and lose the understandings or abilities of any birth potentials, and the practicing of them will not only be more difficult, but any of these natural abilities will be hidden until healing occurs.

The polarities of the four directions will influence each other as the wheel turns. The opposing forces balance and seek harmony with each other, because their place on the wheel complements the opposite pole. Therefore, the new beginning seeks completion, the expanding and growing seeks rest and recuperation.

BELOW

Winter is the time of the North Wind and the time when the Earth rests in preparation for spring. During the Winter Solstice, Grandmother Moon is at her greatest strength. This is when we should ask the elders for knowledge and wisdom.

CYCLES OF THE MOON

T he cross that is formed from east to west and north to south is the solar structure of the Earthweb. These days are more or less fixed, unlike the moon's rotation, which is fluid throughout the cycles of the days, years, and seasons. Her changing faces create subtle influences upon the Earth. In order to help you to walk the Earthweb, you need to refer to the moon calendar at the back of this book, which will give you the position of Grandmother Moon on the day of your birth—your "sun day." This creates your wheel of birth, which will be a strong influence throughout your life.

THE MOON ON YOUR WEB

The medicine wheel is basically a sun wheel. It uses the path of the sun through a day and a season as its template. It shows us the four powers related to the sun and the four winds that are caused by and controlled by the sun.

But the sun has its opposite, the moon, and unless we can place the moon upon the wheel, it will not be balanced. And, as mentioned earlier in the Preface, the Earthweb is all about finding a balance.

Although the moon on your "sun day" is important, you also need to look at where the moon is now on your web. This will guide you on your developing journey around the wheel. You will begin to see a picture emerging—Earth signs—that will show you the

patterns or strands of the web that make up your personality and pathway through this lifetime. You will begin to see your strengths and weaknesses, the reasons that things happen certain ways in your life, and you will discover where your gifts are.

THE MOON CYCLE

The moon, in the course of its own 28-day cycle, goes from its weakest at the new moon to its peak at the full moon, whence its power diminishes again. The moon grows in power as it waxes and decreases in power as it wanes, so the weakest time of any of the moons is as it gets close to the end of one part of its cycle and the influence of the next phase is beginning to rise.

The new moon is thus influenced by the power of the previous full moon and the power of the coming

ABOVE
A Mimbres-style image of two people representing the opposite phases of the moon and the world. Death and rebirth; rest and rejuvenation.

ABOVE
*Radiant Moon by Robert Hughes. The moon
has often been depicted as feminine and linked
to fertility—the menstrual cycle being
associated with a lunar cycle.*

Natoas headdress worn by Sacred or Holy Woman in the Blackfeet Sun Dance. The headdress symbolized power acquired through ceremony.

full moon. This is similar to the conventional signs of the zodiac: if you are born on the cusp—at that time when one sign is changing into the next sign—then you will have the influence of both signs in your birth chart.

The four full moons that coincide with the four winds on the medicine wheel are consistent with those powers on the wheel. The people who are born close to these four moons will be influenced by these powers, thus it is possible to read their propensities by looking at the characteristics of the four winds. The closer these individuals are born to those nodal points, the stronger the wind's influence will be upon their characters.

THE WIND AND YOUR CHARACTER

If you are born on the full moon closest to the Spring Equinox, the influence of the East will be very dominant; the farther you travel away from that moon, the more its influence weakens and is replaced by the influence of the South. If you are born on the full moon closest to the Summer Solstice, the influence of the South will be very dominant; the farther away your birthday is from that moon, the lesser its influence—and so it goes on through the turning of the year.

If you are born on the day before the spring full moon, then your character will be strongly influenced by the East, but there will be a hint of the North as well. The power of the moon and its

influence in your life is, in turn, influenced by where it appears on the medicine wheel in relation to the four directions.

GRANDMOTHER MOON'S 12 MONTHS AND FOUR FACES

We will use 12 months to represent the cycles of the Earthweb. Each moon phase begins on the eleventh of the month and ends on the tenth of the following month.

(There are in fact 13 moons in a calendar year, but because we use a calendar with 12 months in it, it would lead to great confusion to put 13 movable moons within 12 fixed months. We will not ignore the thirteenth moon though, because it has great significance; this is the Blue Moon and will be explained shortly.)

Looking at where the moon actually is on its cycle during that moon month will give clarity to the influences during that period.

If your birthday falls upon the eleventh of any month, your new moon will be influenced by two full moons: you will have the full power of the phase you have just left and will have the rising awareness and power of the phase you are just about to enter.

Each phase includes the four faces of Grandmother Moon—the new moon, waxing moon, full moon, and waning moon. You may like to give thanks to Grandmother Moon sometimes, without asking her for anything in return. The time to do this is during the power of the full moon. All you need to

A ceramic panel on the outer walls of the New Basilica at Villa de Guadalupe depicts the cosmic symbology of the sun and the moon. The church was built to celebrate a vision of the virgin by an Indian in 1531.

do is come from your heart, from that place that feels things. You can do it as often as you like, even once a month at each full moon. This is entirely up to you.

THE CHART

When we look at the circle of the year, we see four clear divisions or four quarters; so within these quarters we will place the 12 moons, three in each.

In plotting the moons throughout a year, we start at the beginning of the year, the place of birth–spring, with the full moon closest to the Spring Equinox; that is the first strong moon of the year.

The moons move upon the wheel because the place of the particular moon will change from year to year; unlike the signs of the zodiac, which have definite starting and ending dates, the moons cannot be fixed rigidly upon the wheel.

This makes perfect sense. The moon controls the water and water flows. Trying to contain water takes its energy away; it becomes stagnant. Try to fix the moons to the medicine wheel, and their power will be lost. It is the same with woman. Try to keep her "contained," stop her natural flow, and you will deprive yourself of her wisdom and power.

When these moons are drawn onto the wheel, you can begin to see the web developing. The opposing months have connections, the four corners have connections, and it is the making of all these connections and others that brings to light the Earthweb.

Bringing it to light is only the beginning though. Remember, bringing into the light belongs in the East, the place of beginnings. We must use this enlightenment and work with it until we have learned its wisdom, until we have brought it into the North.

SPRING MOONS OF THE EAST WIND

People born between February 11 and May 10 will be of the spring moons' time, and the time of strongest power during this period will fall on the Spring Equinox, which is the actual day of the East Wind. The East Wind travels right

ABOVE
A sandstone spire reminiscent of Canyon de Chelly's Spider Rock, lair of the Navajo Earth goddess, Spider Woman.

through the center of the full moon that is closest to the actual day of the Spring Equinox.

The three phases of the spring moons' time–the time of the infant–are the Strong Winds Moon, the Fast Waterflow Moon, and the Planting Moon. These three phases will be influenced in different ways by the power of the East Wind.

When we enter the Strong Winds Moon, we are just coming to the end of the wintertime. So we have the full power of the wisdom and understanding of the North carrying us forward into the dawning time of the enlightenment of the East. There will be a gradual increase of innocence and a sense of new beginnings during this moon's cycle.

We then enter the Fast Waterflow Moon, and it is during this moon time that the power of the East Wind is at its strongest. Here, there will be double the intensity where the full moon and the day of the equinox fall roughly in the same place, which will increase the power of the moon at this time as well. The full moon around this time will be a time of innocence and youth and lightness of being.

But because everything has two sides to it, the double intensity can mean that we become needy or difficult (like a demanding infant) and will need to be careful to remain in balance.

Then we move to the waning moon time of the East Wind,

A Plains Cree shield carrying a typical vision-derived design with the central figures of the sun and the moon, protective and inspirational figures for its owner.

which happens during the Planting Moon. Here we have the fading influence of the East Wind and the beginnings of the rising of the South Wind, so the cycle is turning from the time of light to the time of growth. This moon phase will reflect a time to build and to expand because we realize and see what it is that needs to be done in order to move us forward.

SUMMER MOONS OF THE SOUTH WIND

Then we move to the summer moons' time of the South Wind— the time of the child—when the sun is at its strongest during the cycle of a year. The moons of this time fall between May 11 and August 10, with the solstice falling in between.

The three moon phases are the Flowering Moon, the Drying-Up Moon, and the Hot Winds Moon. The first phase, or the Flowering Moon, will carry the rising influence of the South Wind. This means that we will have the fullest experience of the East Wind behind us and, at the same time, the rising influence of the South Wind in front of us. So, having begun on the new stage (day, year, life, and so on), we now need to begin to understand how to progress with it, or how to be creative, enthusiastic, and full of life.

During the Drying-up Moon the South Wind is at the height of its powers; then with the Hot Winds Moon, the South Wind wanes and the West Wind rises.

FALL MOONS OF THE WEST WIND

Moving west will take us to the three phases of the moon that lie with the West Wind. The West is the time to face our fears, to go within and face what we are afraid of. Winter is coming, and we must be prepared for what lies ahead, and the best of the summer has gone and we need to work at bringing in our supplies, or work at bringing in what we need for the time ahead.

The moons of the West Wind run from August 11 to November 10. These three phases work in much the same way as the others in that we will have a waxing (increasing) time during the first quarter of the West, which is the Hunters Moon, then we reach the full power of the West during the Ripening Moon and the falling away (waning) of the influence of the West Wind during the time of the Harvest Moon.

We are moving gradually away from the summer and into the fall–the time of the adult.

In the Hunters Moon time, there will be a gradual fading of the power of the sun and a gradual increase of the powers of the moon as the days get shorter and the nights get longer. The spring and the fall are times of equality, of more or less equal days and nights. During the Hunters Moon, we are aware of an increasing need to gather things to us, to hunt for what we need, and to begin to harvest the abundance of the summer.

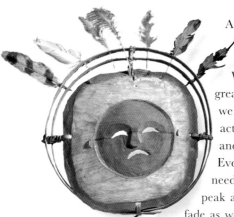

ABOVE

*An Inuit mask
replete with
cosmological
symbolism. The face
is the spirit of the
moon, the border
the air, the hoops
are supernatural
worlds, or levels of
the cosmos, and the
feathers are stars.*

As we move into the Ripening Moon, the West Wind has its greatest power, and we are in the full activity of harvesting and gathering. Everything that we need has reached its peak and will begin to fade as we enter the time of the Harvest Moon. During the Harvest Moon, we will have the awareness of what we have needed to do in order to prepare ourselves for the winter, but will begin to recognize the need for wisdom and understanding, as the West Wind fades and the North Wind begins its gradual rising influence on this part of the wheel.

WINTER MOONS OF THE NORTH WIND

We now move to the time of the North Wind and to the three phases of the moon that fall under the influence of the North. The North Wind is the time of the elder, the time when we try to understand where we are, how we got there, why we are there, and what we should consider doing next. The three moons of the North Wind run from November 11 to February 10 and these are the Popping Trees Moon, the Hard Freeze Moon, and the Deep Snows Moon.

During the Popping Trees Moon, there will be the rising influence of the North Wind.

There will be an increasing awareness of the need to be wise.

During the Hard Freeze Moon when the Winter Solstice occurs, we will have the time of the strongest moon of the winter months, when she will be at the peak of her power. This will be the time when we will be at our full awareness of the need to be thoughtful and wise.

When we move into the Deep Snows Moon, we have the gradual fading of the North Wind's influence and the gradual increase in power of the sun, as the wheel turns toward the dawning of enlightenment and overpowers the moon, to bring light back upon the Earth. The wheel of the Earthweb has turned full circle.

To give you an example, if you were born near to the new moon of winter or the new moon of summer, it will show you the influences from the one before and the one after—as it does in traditional astrology. If you were born early in the full moon of the Spring Equinox, you will have a hint of understanding and enlightenment, but may have weaknesses in bringing things to a conclusion; or, if it worked, have very little idea how it worked.

If you were born closer to the Winter Solstice, you are going to be in the moon time more than if you were born closer to the Summer Solstice. You will be aware of pitfalls and be aware of how to do something without harm or difficulty arising, whereas if you were born during the summer months, you may have little or no awareness of the damage that you may do by your actions because you have not thought things through properly, but you will have great enthusiasm and be fun to be with. Everything on the Earthweb works together to find the balance.

EQUINOXES AND SOLSTICES

The moon represents the dark and the night while the sun represents the light and the daytime. Looking at the cycle of a year, the light and dark are in balance at the time of the two equinoxes in spring and fall. These two points are not fixed but occur around March 21 and September 21. They are the East and the West on the wheel.

South and North are the times of opposites, and at these times we can see the interaction between Grandfather Sun and Grandmother Moon.
The power of the sun is male and causes the winds to blow; the power of the moon is female and causes the waters to flow.

The strongest day in a year for the sun is the Summer Solstice (approximately June 21) and the Winter Solstice is its weakest day. Conversely, the strongest day in a year for the moon is the Winter Solstice (approximately December 21) and its weakest day is the Summer Solstice.

The Winter Solstice on the medicine wheel is in the North, the place of wisdom. The moon is at its strongest at this time so the power of the moon and of woman lives in the North, the place of wisdom. Western civilization has tried to take away the power of woman through domination and fear, but in doing so, they have deprived themselves of the wisdom of woman. Life comes from the woman, she is the one who travels from the North to the East to give life. She is the one Western civilization has forgotten how to pay honor to. Honoring does not mean putting up on a pedestal, here it means acknowledging that men and women have an equal amount to learn from one another.

LEFT
A Tsimshian shaman's storage chest for his religious paraphernalia. The carved face represents the moon. Northwest Coast stories tell of Raven's son breaking open a box containing the moon, which then escaped into the sky.

The 13 Moons

FAST WATERFLOW MOON
March 11–April 10

BIRTHDATE *March 11–April 10*
SEASON *Spring*
WIND INFLUENCE *Eagle*
DIRECTION *East*
ELEMENT *Air*
MOON TOTEM *Hawk*
PLANT TOTEM *Red clover*
MINERAL TOTEM *Clear quartz*
COLOR *Yellow*
COMPATIBLE PARTNERS *People of the fall moons,
especially those of the Ripening Moon.*

ABOVE
*Clear quartz
represents this
moon's energies
because it can
enhance and clarify.*

This is fast waterflow time; the
time of the thaw. It is the time
when the Earth begins to come
out of her slumber, when *Waziya's*
power is overcome by the sun.
This is the time of equal day and
night, when the waters of the
Earth begin to flow swiftly to bring
the water for the seeds that have
endured the frosts, enabling them
to spring forth and send their roots
out in preparation for sprouting
their tender leaves and new shoots.
This is the time of beginnings: the
beginnings of spring, the dawning
of the light and of new growth. In
the time of spring on the wheel of
the year, it is the time of the
infant on the wheel of life and the
time of the East Wind. The East
Wind will be strongest during this

Trifolium   Treeflet Treffles

LEFT
*Red clover is the
plant totem for the
Fast Waterflow
Moon. It forms part
of kinnick-kinnick,
cleaning up and
enhancing the taste
of the other
ingredients.*

moon phase because of the Spring Equinox. Its strength has been building since the waning of the North Wind, and it is now ready to rise, to bring the light onto the earth once more after the hard freezes and long, cold nights.

BEGINNING AND COMPLETING

People of the Fast Waterflow Moon will be sensitive to new beginnings, to the dawning of enlightenment, and will carry an innocence and clarity with them throughout their lives. Like the newborn infant, they need to be recognized and cared for

sometimes. They are able to bring things into being, to start new projects and be inspired by new ideas. The potential weakness with all spring moons' people, including the Fast Waterflow Moon folk, will be to learn how to complete tasks they have begun, and how to maintain consistency throughout any projects without rushing off to start on the next wonderful idea. Fast Waterflow Moon is most compatible with its opposite, the Ripening Moon (September 11– November 10); those people will be able to help Fast Waterflow people to learn how to harvest their efforts, how to maintain a

BELOW
Beautiful spring flowers bursting forth in the shadow of the Tatoosh Mountains in Washington State. This is the moon when things come to life again after the long, cold nights.

balance between beginnings and completions, and to see the value of consistency and persistence. People of the fall moons are givers, and will be able to give the spring moons' people a lot of what they need in order to progress upon their wheel of life. Being opposites, there may be times when there is conflict as the two opposing poles seek harmony and balance with each other, but the potential for growth on both sides is worth bearing in mind. Before spring moons' people decide to leave to start on another new relationship—because you find it easier to begin rather than complete—try to listen to the lessons of the West. This will help you blossom into a complete and less dependent, or naïve, personality and will be very helpful to your personal growth around the wheel of your life.

THE HAWK

The moon totem for Fast Waterflow Moon people is the hawk. Like eagle, owl, or any other raptor, it is a clear-seeing creature, but it is also a creature that has a behavior that has to do with this time of year as well as this time of life. The hawk flies high and is quite often seen circling or soaring, looking for prey; the majority of the time, however, the hawk will be sitting on a tree or perch, somewhere where it can be still and see. In the beginnings, we do not see as clearly as we would like. The hawk is showing us the opposite of its power. It is often difficult to see in the dawning light,

but the hawk sees very well, and when it gets started at something, when it leaves the perch, it only does so when there is a reason to move. An infant is much the same; it acts out of need and cries when it needs to be tended to.

The hawk acts only out of need. It doesn't really fly for the joy or fun of it; it flies because of its need to eat, to get from one place to another, or to find shelter. This is how we should act toward an infant: to fulfill what they need in that moment. The hawk lives this way, and Fast Waterflow Moon people can learn much from it.

PLANT AND MINERAL

Red clover is the plant totem for this time of year; it is one of the first of the early spring plants to come into bloom. It is much the same as mullein, and it is used in *kinnick-kinnick*, the sacred smoke that comes from the pipe. It is one of the ingredients that we blend for use in the pipe and it provides not only a sweet taste in the smoke, it also clarifies, cleans up, and enhances the taste of the other substances in *kinnick-kinnick*.

Clear quartz is the mineral totem for the moon at Fast Waterflow time. This crystal is clear and bright and sparkling, and has the ability to absorb and reflect the light. Clear quartz can be programmed to enhance and clarify, so it is a good representative of the energies of this time of year.

The color of the East is yellow, the color of the rising sun.

ABOVE
Spring sees the thaw and the watering of
the seeds of growth in preparation for the
new beginning.

PLANTING MOON
April 11–May 10

BIRTHDATE *April 11–May 10*

SEASON *Spring*

WIND INFLUENCE *Eagle*

DIRECTION *East*

ELEMENT *Air*

MOON TOTEM *Beaver*

PLANT TOTEM *Dandelion*

MINERAL TOTEM *Citrine*

COLOR *Saffron*

COMPATIBLE PARTNERS *People of the fall moons, especially those of the Harvest Moon.*

LEFT
Citrine is the mineral totem for the Planting Moon because it carries the colors of the East and the dawning color of orange to draw in the rising wind of the South.

This is the time of planting, of preparing the soil to take the seeds that will provide us with the food we need to take us through the coming year. It is the time to leave the dependency of the infant and move to the next part of the cycle. During the spring, as the waters begin to slow enough in this moon of planting, the soils will be rich and full of the moisture that is necessary to nourish new growth.

People of the Planting Moon will be able to see the value of preparing well for each new project, because they will be influenced by the passing moon of the East—the moon of preparation and of new beginnings.

Planting Moon people will not be afraid of hard work and can put a great deal of effort into anything they turn their mind to. They will also have a sense of the necessity to build upon an idea, and will begin to comprehend the need for expansion and effort in order to allow for the fresh new growth. Planting Moon people will be excellent at promoting new ideas, and will bring enthusiasm to any tasks they undertake. They are very much people of the light.

Planting Moon people need a balance which comes from air and water. Like their animal totem, the beaver, they can thrive living close to rivers and streams, but need to feel the fresh air of open countryside in order to be completely

RIGHT
Totemic beaver design from the Northwest Coast. The industrious beaver begins its work around now, and beaver-people are not afraid of hard work and long hours.

at peace. The potential weakness of Planting Moon folk is laziness or confusion about goals. This is not because they are wanting to be lazy, but rather because they sometimes need to be shown what needs to be done or accomplished before they can put their heart and soul into it. The adage of "if you don't know what to do—do nothing" may spring up here. Planting Moon people would benefit from the clarity that meditation or visualization brings, in order to remain clear about what needs to be done to achieve their long-term goals.

Planting Moon people are most compatible with their opposite—the Harvest Moon (October 11–November 10). Harvest Moon people can help Planting Moon folk to plant the right seeds for their life path, because Harvest Moon people can see what is needed at times when those of the Planting Moon may not.

THE BEAVER

Beaver is the animal that represents the moon totem for this time of year. The beaver-person is someone who needs to come out into the world at this time of the year to find what they need to repair, prepare, or build up; to begin a growing of things.

The beaver is an industrious creature and is very much involved in activity now. It comes out of semi-hibernation

BELOW
Coltsfoot is one of the earliest spring flowers and is often found in use as herbal tobacco.

ABOVE
*Beautiful bursts of spring color at National
Monument, Arizona. The Planting Moon
is the time to prepare the ground for the
seeds that will provided for the coming year.*

and begins going onto the land now, whereas during the winter it would only go into the water just enough to reach what it needed below the ice to feed itself. During the spring, as the waters begin to slow, the beaver goes out to mend its lodge and repair the dam, so that the waters will be rich with plants and life. The beaver takes what it needs to make a better swimming place and a better hunting place.

Beaver-people excel at trying to begin new projects. To prepare for the planting and for the summers to come, for growing to be able to take place. Beavers work very industriously through the daylight, but also work very hard into the evening. Their day starts before the sun rises and finishes after the sun sets. They are very active all through the day, but are not afraid to work in the dark. Beaver-people are not afraid of hard work and will put in long hours.

PLANT AND MINERAL

The plant totem for this time of year is the dandelion. Legend says that the dandelion was formed by the dust that was raised from the passing chariot of the sun. Its bright yellow flowers open at dawn and close just before dusk. Dandelion is one of the first plants to appear in the spring. It matures early, giving us fresh greens and

medicines at a time when vegetation is scarce. Because of its strength at this time of the year, dandelion can withstand many adverse conditions, a late frost or a late windy day, without being harmed by them. It is strong this time of year. We can make a cleansing medicine using the leaves and root of the plant, or can eat the greens, cooked or raw, as an addition to our food.

The mineral totem for the Planting Moon is citrine. A blend of yellow and orange, it carries the colors of the East and the dawning color of orange to draw in the rising wind of the South. Citrine can produce the willpower necessary to achieve your goals.

The color is saffron. Often worn by holy men, saffron can build the energy in a gentle and sensitive way, filling you with life.

LEFT
Dandelion is the plant totem for the Planting Moon; it is used medicinally wherever it grows in the world.

LEFT
A Tlingit carved frontlet plaque inlaid with abalone. It represents a beaver with a frog between its paws.

FLOWERING MOON
May 11–June 10

BIRTHDATE *May 11–June 10*

SEASON *Summer*

WIND INFLUENCE *Mouse*

DIRECTION *South*

ELEMENT *Fire*

MOON TOTEM *Deer*

PLANT TOTEM *Fruit and nut trees*

MINERAL TOTEM *Coral*

COLOR *Orange*

COMPATIBLE PARTNERS *Winter moons' people,
especially those of the Popping Trees Moon.*

ABOVE

Seashell is linked to fertility and can help to calm the emotions; it can assist in attuning to the creative and bountiful forces of the natural world.

This is the Flowering Moon time; the time when the fruit and nut trees come into bloom. Everything is bursting with new life, with the birth of young, and with the joy that new life brings.

People of the Flowering Moon will be people who will be blooming. They seem to flower their entire lives. They exude and bubble and burst forth with energy and beauty. A person born this time of year would make an excellent craftsman or artist. They will always be looking for ways to increase and develop their ideas, always curious about some new project to start, but always in a very artistic and beautiful way. Their creative nature brings enthusiasm to their work and their sparkling company will be appreciated and enjoyed by fellow workers or friends.

The potential weaknesses of Flowering Moon folk are lack of staying power and flightiness. There may be a tendency to skip too lightly over details, over other people, or over life in general. In their enthusiasm, they may forget to "dot the I's and cross the T's," which could lead to problems in the future for any plans or projects they are involved with.

The most compatible partners for Flowering Moon people are from the winter moons, especially those from the time of the Popping Trees Moon (November 11– December 10).

The Popping Tree folk can make sure the Flowering Moon people take time out for themselves, can help them to think before they act or speak, and guide them in the wisdom of knowing when to act and when to wait.

ABOVE
The deer is the animal totem for this moon; it
is now that the deer gives birth and should be
left unharmed to raise its young.

THE DEER

Deer is the animal totem of the Flowering Moon time. This is the time when the deer, who is a very timid, innocent creature, is giving birth to its young and is about halfway through the birthing season. It is coming into the fullness of summertime and we are beginning to have warm days. Deer has a power of birth and growth, but mostly of growth.

Deer provides us with food and clothing. We only take what we need, and we should remember to take only what we need. This is the time of the year when we need to let the deer have time to give birth, to let the offspring grow and mature and have their summer.

The mouse is the totem of the South Wind time which runs from May 11 to August 10 in the cycle of Grandfather Sun. Mouse is busy, active, and curious, and so is very representative of the energies of this time of the year.

PLANT AND MINERAL

The fruit and nut trees are strongest at this time of year, because it is the time they come into flower. The time of the cherry, apple, and peach blossoms, and the flowering of the nut trees like pecan, hazel, and beech, reminds us of the harvest that will come later in the year. It reminds us of the abundance that is to come if we tend the soil correctly and keep nourishing the trees.

Similarly, people of the Flowering Moon need to tend to each moment with care and consideration, keeping their joyful character, but also allowing time for consolidation and prudence.

The mineral totem for this moon is seashell. It is linked to the fertility of this time of year and can help to calm the emotions, therefore helping to balance the flightiness of Flowering Moon people and assisting in attuning you to the natural world's creative and bountiful forces.

The color is orange for vitality and enthusiasm; it bubbles with life and exuberance and can assist when needing to maintain energy at an active and creative level.

BELOW
Henry Farney's Indian Encampment near Denver *captures the fact that this is the perfect time to make the most of the bountiful offerings of the natural life around us.*

DRYING-UP MOON
June 11–July 10

BIRTHDATE *June 11–July 10*
SEASON *Summer*
WIND INFLUENCE *Mouse*
DIRECTION *South: includes the strongest sun day*
on the wheel of the year—the Summer Solstice
ELEMENT *Fire*
MOON TOTEM *Otter*
PLANT TOTEM *Cottonwood tree*
MINERAL TOTEM *Rose quartz*
COLOR *Red*
COMPATIBLE PARTNERS *Winter moons' people,*
especially those of the Hard Freeze Moon.

We are coming to the summer wind day–the Summer Solstice, the strongest day for Grandfather Sun on the wheel of the year. Those born on the solstice itself will have the greatest powers of this part of the cycle.

People of the South can bring joy, happiness, beauty, and frivolousness into a business that may be staid and dry. They can lighten an atmosphere with no problem whatsoever, just by being themselves. Wherever a South-person is, there is a joy for life and a beauty that shines for all to see.

Metaphorically, the South-person, being so childish in nature, might need someone to help them set down a root to reach for the water. They can be unwise about how to deal with things, and have poor understanding of what the consequences of their actions will be.

The most compatible moons are the winter moons' people, especially those of the Hard Freeze Moon. It would be wise to heed the words of the Hard Freeze Moon people, who are best suited to guiding them in the straightest and most suitable direction for their needs. Sometimes the opposite moon will bring disagreements into the Drying-Up Moon's life. Remember that you need help to set down your roots sometimes and could benefit from learning how to listen more carefully to wise advice.

THE OTTER

Within this moon we have otter and the cottonwood tree. The otter is a very playful creature, and just as the mouse of the South represents the sun, so the otter represents the moon. The otter is as innocent and curious as the

ABOVE
An Inuit carving of the playful but resourceful otter, animal totem for this moon.

ABOVE

*The Drying-Up Moon is the moon of the
Summer Solstice, the strongest day for
Grandfather Sun. This sunset over trees
and water reminds us of the joy for life
and beauty that shines forth from people
of the South.*

mouse, but it is bigger and more resourceful in its defense.

The otter does not hide as much as the mouse, and it thoroughly enjoys everything that it does. It is a lover of its food, and it is a lover of the way it acquires things; and because most of its food comes from the water, the otter loves swimming and coursing and playing around in the waters where it lives most of its life. In fact, the otter loves everything that it does.

PLANT AND MINERAL

The plant totem for the Drying-Up Moon is the cottonwood tree. This is a very strong tree at a time when the waters are drying up rapidly. We have to have water; it is the blood of life, both on Mother Earth and within ourselves. The person of the Drying-Up Moon is much like the cottonwood tree: they are beautiful to behold, but no matter how much beauty is around them or how frivolous their natures, they have a very deep root and a deep

awareness of the need to understand. The cottonwood tree shows you the source of life and the source of water in what seems like an arid landscape. In the time of dryness, when water is becoming scarce, it shows us where the water is. Because wherever there is a cottonwood tree, there is water.

The mineral totem that represents Grandmother Moon at this time of the year is rose quartz. Rose quartz is the stone of the heart and the stone for healing flaming emotions, so that there is a calm and a balance restored during this highly active time of the year.

The color is red. The color of passion, energy, and enthusiasm. The expansive nature of red can be destructive if it's not put with softer colors sometimes, so blend your reds with pinks and blues and greens in order to prevent burnout.

LEFT
The otter loves the water, both for playing and hunting. It is very capable and has a joy for life.

ABOVE

*Plains Indian men smudging themselves in
sacred smoke and cleansing their bodies as
part of a ceremony. The Sun Dance, held at
the height of Grandfather Sun's powers, is
still a major feature of Plains cultural life.*

HOT WINDS MOON
July 11–August 10

BIRTHDATE *July 11–August 10*
SEASON *Summer*
WIND INFLUENCE *Mouse*
DIRECTION *South*
ELEMENT *Fire*
MOON TOTEM *Trout*
PLANT TOTEM *Thistle*
MINERAL TOTEM *Jade*
COLOR *Green*
COMPATIBLE PARTNERS *Winter moons' people, especially those of the Deep Snows Moon.*

We are now in the moon of the Hot Winds; the time when everything is ripening into maturity. Hot winds are necessary now, because we are coming into the latter part of the growing time. It is the end of the childish time, and the hot winds are needed to help bring things to fruition, to make the seeds come to ripeness.

People of the Hot Winds Moon are very versatile. They fit in, in a lot of different places. The person of the Hot Winds time can blow very hot and have a short temper, but they also have a maturity about them. They can look within themselves to find the answers they need and are resourceful when they are wanting to find out something of value, even though on the surface they may seem to be having a lot of fun.

Potential weaknesses of the Hot Winds Moon people can be giving up too easily, or, conversely, not letting go when it would be prudent to do so. They can be stubborn and should guard against anger, arrogance, or superiority. They could learn to give without conditions attached and be more serious sometimes.

The most compatible partners for Hot Winds Moon folk are the winter moons' people, especially the Deep Snows Moon (January 11–February 10). Deep Snows Moon people can help to balance the active with the peaceful, the resting with the moving and the thinking with the resourceful. They can help the Hot Winds Moon people to dig deep into their own inner wisdom and help to bring out the maturity that Hot Winds

ABOVE
Thistle, the plant totem for Hot Winds Moon, symbolizes the beginnings of coming to maturity, the moving away from the time of the child into the time of the adult.

RIGHT
*Trout, the animal
totem for Hot
Winds Moon, is at
its strongest at this
time of year because
the seeds are just
beginning to fall into
the streams and
rivers and the
trout feeds well.*

Moon people feel within but may have trouble manifesting.

THE TROUT

Trout is the animal totem for the Hot Winds Moon. Trout is strong at this time of the year. It is a game fish, because it is good at putting up a fight whenever it is hooked on a line. It is elusive and wily and knows its territories very well. Trout are strongest at this time of year because the seeds are just beginning to fall into the streams and rivers.

Trout is a very gregarious fish, and Hot Winds people are very gregarious people. They are still outwardly as simplistic and innocent as children, but they are coming into the time of the West Wind and so into the time of the adult. Hot Winds people are starting to be a little more sensible, and the trout is that way. It is very sensible about where it lives and about its ways of swimming. It can swim against the stream, waiting for its food to come to it. It is very playful, or at least it makes people playful as they try to outwit and catch it. To catch a trout is a challenge. Although the trout is a game fish, it is not like the pike. When you catch a trout, you don't have to work too hard to get something decent to eat from it. It is a fine meal and is very versatile in the way that it can be prepared for eating.

PLANT AND MINERAL

The plant totem for the Hot Winds Moon is the thistle. Medicines and food can be prepared from thistles (and others from the nettle family) that can be used in a variety of ways.

BELOW
*The dry heat, amply
evident here in the
wind-eroded
landscape of the
American
Southwest, brings
potency to the time
of the Hot
Winds Moon.*

ABOVE
Mount Rainier National Park in Washington,
a state with an abundance of forests. The
color for this time of year is green; it
represents nature coming into maturity.

The thistle is strong and requires an immense amount of heat to help to bring it into its full glory, because this is the time of year when the thistle blooms and throws its seed.

And so during the Hot Winds Moon we have a plant that is a symbol of virility and strength. This plant symbolizes the beginnings of coming to maturity; the moving away from the time of the child into the time of the adult. The thistle provides us with a lot of things that we need, but it is very serious about the fact that it does not want to give up its food too easily. Reach out and grab one and see if it doesn't bite!

The mineral totem for the Hot Winds Moon is jade. Jade has virile and strong characteristics, and has long been used as a token of male potency. Because this is the time of year when life is wanting to spread its seed, and because of its association with strength and power, jade can help Hot Winds Moon people maintain a balance and equilibrium, sustaining them as they try to handle the fiery and powerful energies of this time of the year. Jade will help Hot Winds Moon people to express their inner feelings and assist them in giving out the best of their personal power–unconditional love.

The color for this time of year is green. The color that represents nature coming into maturity and a balanced heart. Hot Winds Moon people can be hot-tempered when they are out of balance, and the color green can help to soothe tense nerves and the fretful thoughts that overactivity can sometimes produce.

ABOVE

A salmon rattle containing an effigy of a Tlingit shaman. Like the trout, the salmon is a strong and challenging fish at the height of its powers at this time of year.

HUNTERS MOON
August 11–September 10

BIRTHDATE *August 11–September 10*
SEASON *Fall*
WIND INFLUENCE *Thunderbird*
DIRECTION *West*
ELEMENT *Water*
MOON TOTEM *Wolf*
PLANT TOTEM *Lodge pole pine*
MINERAL TOTEM *Blue turquoise*
COLOR *Turquoise*
COMPATIBLE PARTNERS *People of the spring moons,
especially those of the Strong Winds Moon.*

ABOVE
*Blue turquoise brings
great clarity; the
color of the oceans
and tranquility, it is
one of the greatest of
all the healing
stones.*

We are leaving the summer and are at the beginnings of fall. We move more solidly into the time of the adult. The adult is a harvest of maturity, and this is the time of year when we come out of the childish playfulness into something more developed. We begin to notice the shortening of the days as we leave the power of the sun and enter the lengthening of the nights–the power of the moon. This is the time of the waning sun. You are starting to move away from the influence of the male and closer to the influence of the female. We are moving into the time of equality; the time of equal days and equal nights. The people of the Hunters Moon are moving toward the female and as such will have deep insights and intuition to offer. They are people of the fire but are also beginning to be aware of the need for more balance. Here are the people who know how to begin to bring things to a conclusion.

Potential weaknesses of the Hunters Moon people include the need to learn how to look within and claim their power–to learn how to work toward the next part of the cycle now that the harvest is about to be gathered in.

To trust the inner voice and act upon it can sometimes be difficult because, in Hunters Moon folk, the maturity is not quite ripe. They need to guard against flippancy and could learn tolerance when things are not going the way they would like or the way they think they should.

Hunters Moon people recognize the need for the group. They can work well as part of a team, but have a tendency to be solitary at times when it is not always beneficial for them to do so.

The most compatible partners are from the spring moons' time, especially the Strong Winds Moon (February 11–March 10). The balancing of the opposite moon will bring a focus and a clarity that will help Hunters Moon folk to maintain their sense of purpose.

THE WOLF

Wolf is the animal totem for this time of year. Wolf is a very strong power; it is the teacher and the pathfinder–the being that shows the way. People of the West are very powerful people.

The wolf-person is aware of a very frivolous side of themselves, although there are the beginnings of an awareness to grow into adult stature. Wolf is the hunter. It knows how to stalk and gather to it what it needs and has a sense of what will happen at the end. It can spend days and days hunting and only come home with a squirrel, but it has found its food.

PLANT AND MINERAL

The lodgepole pine is the plant totem for the Hunters Moon. At this time of year it is at its full maturity. It can be harvested now to provide the structure of the lodge, so this is the time of year that people begin to recognize the

BELOW
Thomas Dalziel's The Abating Storm *captures the color and element of the Hunters Moon: turquoise and water.*

ABOVE

*A gray wolf howling. Wolf is the teacher and
pathfinder, a strong power that shows the
way. The wolf is also a hunter and knows
how to stalk and gather what it needs.*

need to end the childishness and playfulness and start to be more serious. It is time to cut the tree; time to work steadily at the way to go. It is the time to start to hunt, gather, and put things by; not just the hunting of animals, but the seeking out of what is needed. It is time to begin to look at your own power in the course of the year.

Blue turquoise is the mineral totem for the Hunters Moon. Looking into a blue turquoise is like looking into the spirit of Mother Earth. Blue turquoise brings great clarity and is one of the greatest of all the healing stones; it purifies and cleanses, refreshing the body and soul like a cool shower in a mountain stream. Blue turquoise will help people of the Hunters Moon to maintain a steady balance and to go with the flow; this can mean gathering or letting go. It will help you to know which way to go, as it will enhance your relationship with your own inner voice, the one that knows where you need to be.

The color of this moon is turquoise, the color of the oceans, of healing and tranquility. Turquoise will help you

to dive deeply into yourself without fear, so that you can surface to the maturity of the West–the maturity of the adult, with a clear and balanced view of the future.

ABOVE

A clan-crested dance hat from the Northwest Coast displaying a wolf figure—although it might also be a bear. The potlatch rings on the helmet are hollow and were used to conceal sacred white eagle down which was thrown out by the dancer's head movements. Its scattering was believed to ensure goodwill.

LEFT

A Northwest Coast carved thunderbird totem, the wind influence for this moon.

RIPENING MOON
September 11–October 10

BIRTHDATE *September 11–October 10*
SEASON *Fall*
WIND INFLUENCE *Thunderbird*
DIRECTION *West*
ELEMENT *Water*
MOON TOTEM *Black bear*
PLANT TOTEM *Bearberry*
MINERAL TOTEM *Obsidian*
COLOR *Blue*
COMPATIBLE PARTNERS *Spring moons' people, especially those of the Fast Waterflow Moon.*

ABOVE
Obsidian has divinatory properties; it can allow you to go within yourself to find what you need to take you forward.

RIGHT
A bear totem. During the Ripening Moon, the bear, the animal totem for this moon, isolates itself and cares only for its own needs.

Now we move into the peak moon time of the West Wind–the Fall Equinox. This is called the Ripening Moon time; it is the time of the bearberry and the black bear.

THE BLACK BEAR

The black bear is a very gregarious but solitary creature. It lives and works in very small groups, and since this is the ripening time, it is the time that the bear begins the peak of its activity.

All through the spring and summer, the bear has been getting by. It has been living on fish that it could catch and grubs and insects. But now it is time for the ripening. And as the ripening begins to take place, the berries and nuts start appearing in strength.

The black bear is now putting on its weight in preparation for the winter. It starts isolating itself from others, moving deeper into solitude. It becomes almost egocentric, looking within itself for its own needs, whereas during the time that it was digging for grubs in the summer, when insects and fish were the mainstay, it would work together with others; now it looks only to itself.

The bear fears what is coming, so it begins fighting with other bears and works alone at trying to fatten itself. This is also a tendency of Ripening Moon people, for they can be very solitary and introverted. They are very dark, mysterious people who want to pay a lot of attention to themselves. Ripening Moon people sometimes hide themselves away from both people and busy places.

ABOVE
*This Tlingit Chilkat cloak has a bear design.
The great hunter and salmon catcher, the
grizzly bear was the most important crest
animal among the Northwest Coast cultures.*

ABOVE
The black bear is smaller than the grizzly and is readily found in forested areas. The bear is heavily respected by all Native Americans. To the Cheyenne, the most sacred site on Earth is Bear Butte, east of the Black Hills.

PLANT AND MINERAL

Bearberry is a plant that is used in the making of *kinnick-kinnick*, our sacred tobacco mix. Because of its strength, it is one of the main ingredients I use in the pipe.

Bearberry is a relatively large-leaved bush that produces berries that are rather tart, but they are excellent medicinally. Bearberry makes a good tea for many different ailments, including the breaking of fevers when served hot and strong, or for stomach upsets when the berries are mixed with the leaves to make an infusion.

Like the bear, the bearberry plant will show us what we need as individuals to help us to find our way to help ourselves. This is very much what the people of the West are about—helping themselves.

The Ripening Moon is when things are coming to their peak. After the peak of the West Wind on the Fall Equinox, the time of the West begins fading into winter.

Obsidian has divinatory properties. One can look within the stone and receive information that will be helpful. Because of this, obsidian makes an ideal mineral totem for the Ripening Moon. It can take you within yourself to find the information you need to move forward. Just like the time of the harvest, when you need to know how much to store, where to put it, and how long it will keep.

Obsidian is also a powerful protector. It draws energy that may be harmful away and into itself, making it a stone of great service to its user, and a perfect mirror of the energies of the West.

The color of the West is deep blue. Like the deepest oceans, lakes, and rivers, it is hard to know how far down the waters are flowing and what is moving within them. Ripening Moon folk are also deep, and sometimes they are unfathomable. They feel things very deeply. Therefore the deep blue will bring a calm to any stormy waters, at times when even you are not sure what you are feeling and why.

RIGHT
Bearberry (top) and Green Bearberry (bottom), a good medicinal plant with which to alleviate ailments as well as mix into kinnick-kinnick.

ABOVE
A superb grizzly bear claw necklace from the Fox tribe, which lived on the fringes of the Plains and Great Lakes. Such necklaces were very characteristic of the tribe. Only those men who had made contact with the bear-spirit were qualified to wear one.

HARVEST MOON
October 11–November 10

BIRTHDATE *October 11–November 10*
SEASON *Fall*
WIND INFLUENCE *Thunderbird*
DIRECTION *West*
ELEMENT *Water*
MOON TOTEM *Coyote*
PLANT TOTEM *White ash*
MINERAL TOTEM *Smoky quartz (also called black quartz)*
COLOR *Purple*
COMPATIBLE PARTNERS *People of the spring moons,
especially those of the Planting Moon.*

ABOVE
*Smoky quartz is
excellent for any
psychic journeying
you might take; it
will protect you
from harm and show
you how to release
blocked energy.*

Coyote is the creature that is attributed to many legends for having a playfulness about him. He is the trickster, the clown, the jester. This is the time of the year when we have bright sunny days; we sit and look out at the beautiful days and go running outside in our shirtsleeves, only to find that it is cold and we have to go back inside for warmer clothing. The sun, and even the skies, seem to be making an effort to trick us and fool us into a false sense of pleasure or false expectation of what will be if we go out into it.

THE COYOTE

Coyote is a trickster; he is also a survivor under many, many adverse conditions, and the person born of this time is beginning to grow toward the wisdom of the North, a wisdom that many people would aspire to.

A wisdom of how to use both the light and the darkness. How to hide, yet get the light that is needed. How to live in conditions that seem not to be the coyote's way.

You find coyote living in downtown Los Angeles drinking from the Los Angeles River. You find coyote living in the city of Denver, not up in the mountains, but in the city, because it is there he finds the easiest life. This is also a tendency of the coyote-person: they play, they have fun, they know how far to go, but they also look for an easy way.

This seems to be a contradiction of harvest, because the harvest is a time of intense labor. It is the time of work when people are concentrating on preparation and getting ready for the winter to come. It is the time when you start gathering and putting by and digging pits to put foods away in. Well, coyote does the same thing to some extent. He is a creature that behaves erratically. During the springtime, he will sometimes kill more than he needs to eat (like the fox in England) and it goes to waste. But in the fall, he kills and stores his prey. He will bury it and remember its place, so he can go back. He knows that times are coming when food will be scarce.

PLANT AND MINERAL

White ash is the plant totem for this time of year. It is the equivalent to the rowan tree in England. The rowan grows rather small in stature and in very awkward places–high in the hills, on the edge of the moors, and up in the mountains. It grows in precarious places, and this Harvest Moon is a very precarious place, because it is a place where, if you don't gather enough, you won't make it until the spring. The rowan tree knows how to survive in places where you don't think it is possible.

The white ash grows very differently in North America. It grows into a very large, straight tree. This is the time of the year when the white ash is harvested. Its limbs make the best bows and lance shafts–and this is because the sap has run out of the tree, so it doesn't take much work to shape it into a bow or staff. It gives itself willingly for this purpose, and it works very well with the person who is trying to put it into shape. It gives itself readily for the working that will take place during

the winter when there is a need to make tools and mend things.

And so it is with the Harvest Moon people. They are capable of giving themselves in service to others and of providing for the needs of others. Their potential weaknesses include being too distant or removed from what is going on, so that they miss opportunities to share what they know, or they may have a tendency toward lack of confidence or self-doubt. The best moons to help the

ABOVE
This depicts a scene from the Iroquois story of the thunderers, the people of Iti'nun, who keep the world in order. Here, they have turned a man into a porcupine for trying to kill another young man.

Harvest Moon people are the spring moons, especially the Planting Moon people. These people will help to clear the stagnant waters that may be lurking within a Harvest Moon person, so that they are able to move more rapidly toward an enthusiasm and lightness of being, that will bring the light of understanding into what they must do, or what work they must undertake, in order to know themselves better.

Smoky or black quartz is the mineral totem for this time of the year. Smoky quartz is excellent for use during meditations and visions, or any psychic journeying you may take. It will protect you from harm and show you how to release blocked or stale energies. It helps produce clarity and will draw the energy that you need toward you if you keep it with you. Some forms of smoky quartz have been artificially irradiated to make them dark; look for a natural smoky quartz for use with the Earthweb.

The color for this time of the year is purple. Purple is the color worn regularly by royalty to signify not only a superior birth but also a spiritual wisdom that will guide the people in the ways of truth, justice, and peace. People of the Harvest Moon will benefit from meditating upon the color purple to help them come to terms with the deep and profound feelings they frequently experience, which are often for the benefit of mankind or the Earth we live upon. Purple will help you to be a leader; a pathfinder, without falling into the trap of superiority.

RIGHT
Coyote is a prominent totem figure among Native Americans. For many, he is a Creator figure, a trickster-transformer responsible for many natural and cultural conditions.

ABOVE

*John Kensett's Lake George in 1870. When
selecting a spot to meditate, try to choose one
that is positioned to enable you to draw in
and harness the powers of the natural world
around you; a site overlooking a lake is ideal.*

POPPING TREES MOON
November 11–December 10

BIRTHDATE *November 11–December 10*

SEASON *Winter*

WIND INFLUENCE *Waziya*

DIRECTION *North*

ELEMENT *Earth*

MOON TOTEM *Owl*

PLANT TOTEM *Dandelion*

MINERAL TOTEM *Aquamarine*

COLOR *Indigo*

COMPATIBLE PARTNERS *People of the summer moons,
especially those of the Flowering Moon.*

ABOVE

Aquamarine is the mineral totem for this moon, a feminine stone that can produce inspired thoughts.

This is the Popping Trees Moon time. If you walk through the woods in cold climes at this time of year, you hear the trees "popping" because of the freezing and consequent expansion of the unfallen sap. Very cold times are coming, and the hard frosts are happening now; this is when you can hear many of the trees popping and cracking.

Elm as a tree has become rather scarce because of the Dutch Elm Disease that spread throughout the world. This, too, has a wisdom to it. The elm trees that survived lived in isolated places rather than large groves; they were the ones that had managed to become separated. It was almost as if they chose to be away from their own kind in order to allow for survival. So we watch the elm and recall the lessons that elm can give us for our survival.

So it is with Popping Trees Moon people. Sometimes they need to isolate themselves from the group and take time to withdraw from society in order to emerge with new knowledge and understanding.

THE OWL

Many people consider the owl a creature that only hunts during the night, but those that really know about it know that it hunts in the twilight and at dawn as well. I have kept rescued barn owls, and they have wonderful characters. Yes, they are alert at night, but they are alert because of the activity of the night, not because it is a good time to hunt. The best time for them to hunt is in the dusk, at the setting of the sun. We have come away from the equinox, and this is the active time for the owl. They are difficult to spot, but this is when they are most readily seen. This is the time

LEFT
*The owl is often
seen as embodying
wisdom, for they
know to watch and
wait before acting.*

of year before the deep night, when you can actually see the most owl activity. This is also a creature of feminine power—the power of the moontime.

The owl has very acute hearing. Many people think that because the owl has very large eyes it sees well at night, whereas it works much more from sound. The ears are forward, and the dish-shaped feathers around the eyes help it to hear better. Owls are very wise creatures. They know the wisdom of stopping, waiting, listening, and watching before taking action. They know end results. They know that too

ABOVE
*A beautiful carved and painted Tsimshian
dance object. The charm is shaped like a heart
and opens to reveal the wise owl which
represents the soul of someone who
died recently.*

much activity is going to do a great deal of harm to them, because they are fragile: their bones are virtually hollow, and therefore have a lot of respect for keeping the balance and not harming unduly. The owl works with the wisdom, and so it is with Popping Trees Moon people; they are coming into wisdom's time.

MINERAL AND COLOR

The mineral totem is aquamarine. Like the light in the sky just after the sun has set, this stone has a clear, pale, and ethereal quality, which brings to users an ability to express themselves clearly. It is a very feminine stone that can produce inspiration and inspired thoughts. It can bring the user a lightness and a sense of peace at times when the way forward may be unclear, exactly as it is when the sun has just set.

The color for this time of the year is indigo. Indigo is a hard color to describe. It looks blue, then purple, then it looks black. It could be soft, it could be hard. It is a very deep color; a very mysterious kind of color, just like the people of the Popping Trees Moon. Indigo can help you to fathom your own depths, and to reach for a spiritual understanding about the nature of wisdom in the beginnings of the wintertime.

BELOW
A snowstorm in Canada. The cold and the frost and the snow cause the trees to pop and crack during the time of Waziya.

HARD FREEZE MOON
December 11–January 10

BIRTHDATE *December 11–January 10*
SEASON *Winter*
WIND INFLUENCE *Waziya*
DIRECTION *North—includes the strongest*
moon day on the wheel of the year, the Winter Solstice
ELEMENT *Earth*
MOON TOTEM *White buffalo*
PLANT TOTEM *Hazel*
MINERAL TOTEM *Granite*
COLOR *Saffron*
COMPATIBLE PARTNERS *Summer moons' people,*
especially those of the Drying-Up Moon.

ABOVE

Granite is the mineral totem for the Hard Freeze Moon—strong, tough, and harsh, a powerful protector against the freezing temperatures of winter.

The hazel tree is a tree that gives nuts, but hazelnuts, or filberts, are rather difficult to crack. They give, but they keep at the same time. The hazelnut keeps well–far better than other nuts. You can keep hazelnuts for years, and they will still either bear a sapling or be edible. They can be eaten not just in that season but for many seasons to come. Walnuts do not last for more than a couple of years before they have to be thrown away. But the hazel maintains its strength, retaining its ability to be used as a food far longer than many of the nuts.

The hazel itself is a strong old tree. It doesn't grow so large as to be a rod for lightning. It doesn't grow such a large spread as to be prone to popping and giving up limbs when it is not necessary. It is also a tree where the nuts don't seem to weigh the tree down. Not like the pecan, which gets so heavy with nuts that its limbs can break. They are producing so much that they are harming themselves. This wisdom of knowing just how far to go, knowing how to hold on to their strength and protect themselves, but still share themselves for long periods of time, is part of the hazel's wisdom.

So it is with Hard Freeze Moon people. They have gifts to give and pearls of wisdom to share. They are strong and have a wisdom about them that often seems beyond their years. They can, however, lean toward being too knowledgeable, making comments and remarks at times when it would be more helpful to listen. Hard Freeze Moon people need to learn how to balance wisdom with understanding, listening without

speaking, when to give and when to take. They can sometimes be unclear about what is the right thing to do.

Their most compatible partners are from the summer moons, especially the Drying-Up Moon. Drying-Up Moon folk will help the Hard Freeze Moon people to warm up a little bit, become more compassionate and warmer in nature, helping to color wisdom with love and consideration for the feelings and thoughts of others.

THE WHITE BUFFALO

The moon totem for the Hard Freeze Moon is the white buffalo. We all have a sense of the buffalo and what he means to the Native American people. I'm not talking about the buffalo albinos that are thrown off occasionally, which are pink-eyed and weak and whose skin burns easily, along with many other problems; I am talking about the dark-eyed white buffalo that has a white fur and has the strength of the dark-furred buffalo. It is, however, the rarest of all buffalo–it is scarce and comes only when it is needed.

Our Native American legends talk about the coming of the white buffalo as a portent of something wonderful that will happen. Isn't that wisdom? The wisdom comes as a portent of greatness. We don't have wisdom or an understanding of things without having knowledge, or having a measure of it being something that is good for us. *Waziya* comes along every year, but the white buffalo comes only rarely. Wise people come rarely. Their wisdom is something that comes very sparingly and needs to be sought, and then when it is found, there is a need to honor it, because it is the white buffalo that brings with it the knowing what to do and how to do it.

ABOVE
Blackfoot buffalo stones, or iniskim, used during rituals for calling the buffalo. Most are fossils, but any stone or pebble with an unusual shape might be chosen, given a medicine designation, and kept wrapped in buffalo hair as part of a medicine bundle.

BELOW
A buffalo round-up in South Dakota. An animal once threatened with extinction is today safe.

ABOVE
*A medicine man photographed by Edward
Curtis. Note the buffalo skull, an important
accessory in a number of Lakota ceremonials.
The white buffalo is the moon totem for the
Hard Freeze Moon.*

MINERAL AND COLOR

The mineral totem that represents the moon in this time of the North is granite—strong, tough, and harsh. It has holding qualities, but can still breathe because it is slightly porous. It can withstand extreme temperatures, making it a powerful protector against the freezing temperatures of winter.

The color of the North is white. *Waziya* is the totem of the North Wind. He is the white giant of the North (or Jack Frost as he is known to white European people), and he spreads his sparkling white cloth upon the earth to allow her to sleep under his blanket of frost and snow. This allows time for the seeds to strengthen and endure in order to make sure they are hardy and healthy for the years to come. He brings the conditions necessary for rest and for introspection until the growing time comes again in the season of spring. *Waziya* makes us pull inward, drawing everything we need closer to us, giving us time to consider and contemplate things. In the time of the North Wind this is what we should be doing—being wise as to how we should act, in order to survive.

ABOVE
Joseph H. Sharp's
Spirit of the Buffalo *depicts a ceremony devoted to the Lakota figure, White Buffalo Maiden. Its theme is the affection a father has for his child— pure and without blemish, like the maiden—and that good should come of that affection.*

DEEP SNOWS MOON
January 11–February 10

BIRTHDATE *January 11–February 10*
SEASON *Winter*
WIND INFLUENCE *Waziya*
DIRECTION *North*
ELEMENT *Earth*
MOON TOTEM *Blue jay*
PLANT TOTEM *Poplar*
MINERAL TOTEM *Amethyst*
COLOR *Violet*
COMPATIBLE PARTNERS *People of the summer moons, especially those of the Hot Winds Moon.*

ABOVE
Amethyst is the mineral totem for the Deep Snows Moon; it has long associations with wisdom and purity of thought.

People of the Deep Snows Moon can tend to be rigid in their thinking sometimes, and rather introverted, even depressed occasionally. But they have very upright and honest qualities that make them quietly reliable and responsible during the chaos that comes to us in life sometimes. They have the ability to see their way clearly into the future and so can guide others at times when it is really not perceptible what the outcomes will be.

THE BLUE JAY

The blue jay is a creature that knows what it needs. It is willing to tell you whatever it is that it thinks you should know—and in some senses this is wisdom. The blue jay person has a knowledge and a wisdom, and tends to like to talk about it. The jay is a bird that is vociferous in its telling; so much so, that at times people don't want to listen to it. They don't recognize the wisdom of it, because they hear so much of it, and the person of this moon should guard against becoming just such a person. The problem is that we are coming to the end of the wisdom time and approaching the enlightenment time. The jay is a creature of enlightenment as well; it seeks it because it is a curious creature—and sometimes its curiosity is to its detriment. It might get caught easily by the cat, or another predator that it has, because it tends to be a bit over-confident in its wisdom. Be warned! This creature, in heading toward the light, will sometimes do something so rash that it is harmful to itself.

The wisdom of knowing when to stop is weakening, as the influence of the North Wind is waning to make way for the rising wind of the East—the time of the eagle.

RIGHT
Blue jay knows what it needs, and its curiosity sometimes causes it harm. The bird was central to winter ritual among the tribes of the Plateau region.

Blue Jay male 1
Corvus cristatus
Plant

PLANT AND MINERAL

The poplar tree is a very tall and slender tree, whose limbs reach up to the light out of the darkness. The limbs grow very tall and straight, but they also have a tendency to lean and to fall. They represent this time of year because there aren't any strong winds. It is the time of the deep snows, and the poplars reach up to the light out of that snow. They are strong because of the lack of wind. Have you ever noticed in snowstorms or blizzards, the winds don't seem to come from any one direction? This time of year, that's the way that things are; it is the time when the North, the South, and the East winds are blowing together and swirling. The poplar can stand up to these winds because it does not spread itself wide, but holds itself close, reaching for the light during the time of the snows. We are coming back to the time of enlightenment. Coming out of the darkness, into the light.

The mineral totem for this time of the year is the amethyst. Amethyst has long been associated with wisdom and with purity of thought. But amethyst also carries the light. It is the color of the pale sky just before the dawning. It sparkles and reflects like the sparkling you find on a crisp bed of snow in the sunlight. It has the same qualities; it is crisp and clean. Amethyst can help you to carry the wisdom of the North with you around the wheel to the dawning of the light of the East.

The color for this time of the year is violet. Violet is the highest vibration of light. Violet inspires the mind, increases intuition and idealism, and helps spiritual consciousness to rise. At a time of year when we begin to move into the dawning of enlightenment, violet will ensure that the highest vibrations emerge to stimulate the awakening light within ourselves.

BELOW
The poplar tree is strong because there are no strong winds in any one direction at this time. It holds itself tall and close together, reaching up for the light.

ABOVE

*Arizona's Monument Valley, whose dry heat
reminds us of the Hot Winds Moon and its
people who make the most compatible
partners for those of the Deep Snows Moon.*

STRONG WINDS MOON
February 11–March 10

BIRTHDATE *February 11–March 10*
SEASON *Spring*
WIND INFLUENCE *Eagle*
DIRECTION *East*
ELEMENT *Air*
MOON TOTEM *Goose*
PLANT TOTEM *Willow*
MINERAL TOTEM *Moonstone*
COLOR *Dove gray*
COMPATIBLE PARTNERS *People of the fall moons, especially those of the Hunters Moon.*

ABOVE
Moonstone is the mineral totem for Strong Winds Moon. It represents the mother and can bring about the qualities necessary for caring and nourishing new beginnings and new life.

Now we enter the Strong Winds Moon. The time when the winds are blowing hard and fast.

People of the Strong Winds Moon often have original minds and a sparkling wit, but they can sometimes be so far ahead of the others that they can be misunderstood or ignored. How many of us look up and notice the goose flying back, as it returns to herald the dawning of springtime?

Strong Winds people may need to learn to be consistent and not get blown about by circumstance. Sometimes they could feel isolated, and at those times they should seek out others of the same heart and mind in order to share their spiritual thoughts.

Strong Winds people can also sometimes come across as needy and demanding, because they get lonely when no one notices them. Because they are leaders, they can sometimes come to the end of their tether and need at those times to call upon their inner strength and spiritual insight to see them through their crisis. They are wise and confident if they take the time to get to know their enduring and refreshing qualities. In the time of the Strong Winds Moon, we must learn how to bend with the winds of life in order to come to enlightenment.

THE GOOSE

In the dawning of the East Wind, the goose is coming north now. It is heralding the time that is to come, showing us that there is soon going to be the awakening time. It is time for the spring sun because we see the goose coming, and it is good to see it now because we are reaching the end of our stores. We are coming to the end of what we had put away, and goose provides us with fresh food. Goose is a food of man, providing something fresh when it is most needed–at the end of winter.

PLANT AND MINERAL

Willow is a tree that bends in the wind. It is one of the trees that shows its buds in the springtime. This is the time of year when the willow bark turns a brighter red (or green, depending on what kind of willow it is).

The red willow is also a medicinal plant. The bark from red willow is where aspirin comes from. This time of year, when the bears are coming out, we begin to notice the affinity that the bear has with the willow. The bear is grabbing anything that it can find to eat and quite often gets a stomach upset or a headache. It then goes straight to the willow for its medicine!

The willow branch is very flexible; it is good for bending. This is the tree we Native Americans use to make our medicine wheels and dreamcatchers and sweat lodges.

LEFT
Strong Winds Moon people are leaders, who will exhibit wisdom and confidence if they take the time to get to know their enduring qualities.

ABOVE
Pollarded Willows and Setting Sun *by Van*
Gogh. Willow is the plant totem for this
moon; it buds in the springtime and
its bark turns color now.

Mist rising over the mountains as if to symbolize awakening, as the sun comes into stronger power and the spring replaces the winter.

The willow is also a very good tree to make our medicine shields with.

The mineral totem for this time of the year is the moonstone. It represents the mother and is especially effective for childbirth. In this time of awakening to the light, in this time of awakening to the needs of the infant, when demands must be met, the moonstone can bring about the qualities necessary to care for and nourish our new beginnings or our new understandings about life. Moonstone balances the emotions and helps us to realize exactly what it is that we really need.

The color for this time of the year is dove gray. This is the color of unselfishness; it is deeply spiritual and represents the purest human love that comes from the spirit.

At the rising time of the infant, we need to be soft and gentle with ourselves and take time to be with loved ones and friends, just as we would before the time of the birth of a baby. It is the time to be gentle, and it is the time for the innocent language of the heart to be expressed. The soft gray light that embraces us just before the dawn, the softness of the spirit of dove gray, breathes its dawning of the light into our souls.

THE BLUE MOON

MOON TOTEM *Snake*
PLANT TOTEM *Water reeds*
MINERAL TOTEM *Fool's gold*

The Blue Moon is the thirteenth moon of the year. When there are two moons that fall in the same segment, the second moon is called the Blue Moon. These Blue Moons occur about once every two and a half years, and most frequently in months with 31 days in them. But you never know when it is going to appear without examining a lunar calendar.

ABOVE

The snake is the animal totem for the Blue Moon and should be respected not feared. Be wary of the Blue Moon person, for although they are beautiful in nature, they are volatile in temperament.

It is the snake moon. The snake is a very fearsome creature to many people, and the Blue Moon has power, like the snake, because it doubles the intensity of that part of the year in which it falls; if it is during the East Wind, then people of that time will be much more into new ideas than if only the one moon passed through. It is rather eerie to consider how much better they can see; it is also eerie to consider how little they know about how to finish a project, and how much more they need to be grounded in wisdom because they flit about in very extreme activity. In the East or the South, the Blue Moon can be a very intense energy, because those affected will have all the qualities of those winds–the light, the innocence, the curiosity. They will be perceiving the light but not the darkness, failing to see the balance but needing it.

If the Blue Moon occurs in fall or winter, they could be so introverted or so much in the darkness as to not be able to perceive the light in order to find any benefits.

If the Blue Moon comes with the North Wind, those affected are not necessarily going to be profoundly wise in all things–it could be that they try and flow too much with the waters of life to the point that they never reach the land.

A TIME OF CHANGE

Like a snake, this is difficult to grasp; the snake is also a creature of change, and the Blue Moon heralds a time of great change.

The snake sheds its skin, but in the process of shedding its skin it has great difficulty. Should that shedding not occur and the snake not find what it needs to help it pull the skin away from itself, the change can suffocate and kill it. Therefore, an attempt to change can be the snake's undoing. When it occurs, however, it can be magnificent: just before shedding, the skin is dull and listless and there is no shine to it at all; but when it finishes shedding the dead skin, the snake gleams so brightly that you can see it at night.

There are two sides to everything: there is a benefit and a detriment; so it is a matter of recognizing that the strength of the moon could be a benefit—but it could also be such a strength that it is stifling. It detracts us from making any improvements.

Be wary of the person who is born in the full of the Blue Moon. They are beautiful in nature, but don't tread on them for they tend to be very volatile. The snake is fearsome to behold and needs to be given a lot of respect. Snake should be given a wide berth until you can judge what kind of mood he or she is in, or, indeed, what kind of snake he or she is.

PLANT AND MINERAL

Water reeds are the plant totems for this moon, although sweetgrass can also represent the Blue Moon. Sweetgrass can enlighten and cleanse the atmosphere, but too much can sour the air; it has a double edge to it, too.

Iron pyrites or fool's gold is the mineral totem for the Blue Moon. Real gold is malleable and soft; fool's gold looks as attractive, but when you try to mine it, you find it is sharp and hard. Like the snake, it doesn't give its true meaning in its initial contact. People look at snakes and they fear them; it would be better to respect them. Looking at fool's gold, there is a rush of greed and avarice when one should be more temperate and recognize that it is not what it seems. Working it can hurt you rather than help you. Iron is the solid flesh of Mother Earth, and in this stone it is encased in the golden colors of Grandfather Sun, showing us yet again that this fool's gold is not what it seems.

BELOW
As might be expected, snake associations figure prominently amongst the Native Americans of the southwestern United States. This is a sandpainting of Whirling Snakes.

ABOVE
An animal hide bearing the legend of the snake clan from the Hopi people of the southwestern United States. Before the famous Hopi snake dance, the men gather snakes from each of the four directions.

THE EARTHWEB AND THE HEYOKA WHEEL

There is something that happens when we move from the northern hemisphere to the southern hemisphere of the Earth. Our wintertime is their summertime; our summertime is their wintertime. The influences of the North and South Winds are reversed. This doesn't mean that we put North in the South and South in the North–the direction of North remains going northward and the direction of South remains going southward. It means that we have to change the meanings of the two around, so that the influences of the North Wind take on the meanings and powers of the South Wind and the influences of the South Wind take on the meanings and powers of the North Wind.

Everything on this Earth is fluid and flowing and changing and growing. Nothing is fixed, and many, many times things are not what they seem. Even on this small rock called Earth, there are things that do not fit in where we would like them to. This is *heyoka*, the trickster, the jester–the medicine of nothing being as it seems, of turning things upside down. So if you go to the southern hemisphere, or anywhere that is below the equator, then you have to reverse the meanings that we have for North and South.

The directions and meanings of East and West remain the same, because the sun still rises in the East and sets in the West all around the world.

CHOOSING YOUR PERSONAL STONES AND TOTEMS

You don't so much choose your totems as they choose you. But the way you learn about them is to learn about the natural life of the trees or of the animals; learn about how their lives are reflected in ours. *Mitakuye oyasin*–we are all related. Find out the ways in which we are related and maybe the ways the totems are reflected in our own lives. Learn about the things in your own life that need to be filled in order to be more fulfilled in a more circular nature, more in the circle, in the completeness, of this Earthweb, and look for that totem that would give you the lessons that you need. In calling to these totems–and there are many ways to call to them–I myself use sage and sweetgrass. I also use a variety of ceremonies that aren't always the ones that I was taught specifically as ceremonies for these things, but the ones that I've adapted throughout my life to fit.

I have based them not only on the learnings that I have, but also firmly upon the life that I have lived and my individual seeking for power and knowledge and whatever it is that I needed to have in my life.

If you go to look at these things, you have to look at it from your own life and your own life experiences. That's one of the reasons why we can never criticize religions, or rather the individuals within a religion, because they are only working with what they know.

Every human being has a different aura, or energy field, that makes him or her unique. In order to honor this individuality, the stones and totems should, ideally, be chosen personally. Stones and crystals may call to you, or you may find one while out walking that speaks with something inside yourself. When collecting stones for your Earthweb, you may also find they arrive as gifts. By using your intuition and believing in what feels right for you, you gather an energy to you that will empower and enable you to walk the wheel in your own unique way.

It is not necessary to know about the conventional meanings

ABOVE

Just as this Lakota warrior is providing for the birds and learning about them, so the natural world around him provides for his people and the circular nature of the Earthweb is readily understood by observing and learning.

or interpretations that have been given to certain stones and crystals. I have had some very profound experiences when I have taken the time to develop my own relationship with any stones that come to me.

You can discover what they mean to your energy field by sitting quietly with one at a time held in your hands and asking why this stone may help you and which position it wishes to take on your Earthweb. If you find it a little difficult to know where to place your stone-people, lay each one out in all four of the directions and find where you feel it rests most comfortably. It may take a little time to have faith in your own intuition and feelings, but if you trust in your inner voice, your relationship with the stones and totems will increase as your intuition is given the freedom to express what is right for you.

In order to help you develop your relationship with the mineral kingdom, it may be helpful to understand that the qualities of certain stones will complement the different energies of the moons within each of the four seasons.

STONES FOR THE SEASONS

For the winter moons, the time of freezing, I choose stones that can withstand the cold and hold the energy by keeping it or storing it. This is the season where you could place your record-keeper crystals,

fossils, or petrified wood (all of which have connections with the elders who have walked upon the Earth before us, and with the ancient wisdom of our ancestors). You may also consider using any stone that brings wisdom and understanding, perhaps an amethyst, for example.

For the spring moons, the moons of renewal, you may like to choose clear, bright, or sparkling stones that reflect the innocence and purity of the new beginning that is represented by the direction of the East.

Summer moons, the moons of the hot winds, can be represented by any stones that enhance or expand creative, warm, and expressive qualities. I have chosen stones that are fiery, or are the colors of fire, because South is the direction of the fire element.

For the fall moons, the moons of harvesting and giving, I have chosen stones that gather or draw the energies for inner and outer development. You can choose stones that are dark in color, or perhaps you may find gifts from the sea, such as pearl or a seashell, to represent water, which is the element of the West; something that will enable you to finish a task or project successfully, which will help you to harvest the fruits of anything you have started. An example of this could be azurite, a crystal that has the ability to draw in the light of truth and cleanse us of things that are no longer relevant. At times of

ABOVE
Your choices for summer's stones should reflect the fiery qualities of the moons of the hot winds.

ABOVE
Harvesting and giving, drawing something to a completion, are the themes of fall, and you should gather stones that you feel embody that.

ABOVE
It is a personal choice, but for the winter moons, fossils seem particularly appropriate.

ABOVE
Spring being a time of renewal, bright, lively stones make a good choice.

completion, or harvest, it is necessary to conclude on every level, and this often means letting go totally of the cycle we have just been a part of.

The stones and totems that choose to be with you initially may well change over time, as you evolve and grow. Stones may disappear as new ones come to take their place, or you may feel that something needs to be changed on your wheel. It is important that you allow your Earthweb to evolve as you yourself

evolve, and to grow and change as you do. If you try to hold on to medicine objects, you will fix your evolution in time, which means you will be working with a power that no longer exists and operating within a memory that is your past. Your stones and totems may change quite regularly.

Your wheel will move on—this is the nature of life on Mother Earth. In order to evolve, humans must remember to trust in the wheel of life as it turns to the next part of its cycle.

BELOW
Many people of the Earth live in a world that others might regard as less seasonal. Those who live in permanent winter in the Arctic, for example, work in detail with the natural life that exists around them, as well as those larger things that we all share in different ways: the sun and the moon.

LAYOUTS FOR THE EARTHWEB

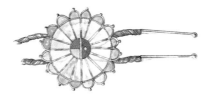

How are you going to use these circles, these webs, these layouts of stones? And how are you going to begin searching for the initial stones to start working with the wheel? In fact, when searching for the animals and the plants—for a lot of things—I have got to emphasize very strongly that the information in Earth Signs is just guidance; that this is a way to examine not the answer, but the question.

HOW THE INDIVIDUAL USES THEM

The uses of the Earthweb are multiple, whether examining the Earthweb in a structure or laying out our stones in their circle. Remember, too, that we don't have to use the stones that we have chosen in this book—we can go and pick up gravel out of the driveway; that will work, because it's not the kind of stone you use that matters, it's the lesson offered by the wheel. It's recognizing and giving honor to, calling to, giving to, and asking from the direction.

VARIETIES OF INTERPRETATION

It is nice to look at the Earthweb, with its semiprecious stones and its trees, and to consider the different plants and the animals, too, but then everyone experiences these things differently. Everyone finds different things. It would not be difficult to examine the life of the jay and find it in the South, instead of finding it in the North.

There is huge variation in interpretation because of people's individual lives, and it is important to recognize that and to show that in this book, because different people see things in different ways.

LOOKING FOR OPPOSITES

All these things are only a guide in order to be able to begin to look at how to understand the examination process, because each person working with the web is going to find different aspects that reflect themselves.

When they start looking at themselves, they should start looking for reflections—because the opposite is the important thing: looking for opposites.

If you're a person who was born in the time of enlightenment, then you need to work with a person who has a sense of completion. If you are a person of a childish nature, then you need to look for a person of a more mature temperament—the wisdom keepers, the elders of the North.

This goes right the way through life, from looking for relationships to looking for partners in a work project or looking for a business partner. You need opposites, and there's that old adage about opposites attracting. Opposites attract for a very good reason, because opposites exist in the same place. If you look in a mirror, you see everything backwards from the way that it is. But it is a perfect backwards, because you are seeing the left on the right and the right on the left–it's a perfect reversal. So when you are looking at the wheel, you also have to look at the fact that everything is a reversal. Thus, if you are looking for enlightenment, if you are looking to the East, you might see enlightenment or you might be the person who is enlightened because you were born in the East–but then again you might be a person who needs enlightenment. This must all be taken into consideration, that sometimes what you are looking for is what you are, and sometimes what you are is what you are looking for!

Always look at the reflection. The Celtic saying of "As above, so below," and the Lord's Prayer "On

ABOVE
Nature in its raw beauty is never less than interesting and frequently awe-inspiring; close observation of it offers lessons for all of us, whether we are scientists or simpler, spiritual folk.

Earth as it is in Heaven," tell of how all things are reflected, and when you find the stones you are finding reflections of your needs. You are finding reflections of what you are and you use them in this way. You might end up with a bag of stones that you use solely for seeking things; you might end up with a bag that you lay out in a ceremony to remind yourself of where you are, or where you were the last time you worked with them. Or you might instead have a circle of stones to seek guidance. It's just a question of working out the ways that you would like to use them.

DIFFERENT USES FOR THE STONES

Earthweb stones can be used for divination. They can be used as a form of celebration or ceremony or prayer. They can be used in working with other people. You can use them as teaching tools or as learning tools. There is the person who holds the bag and has the lessons to help guide others to find their way in the circle, or recognize their place in the circle. So there are all these many ways they can be used; remember, I am not so much giving details of the uses, but just pointing out that they can be used in all these different ways.

There is also a healing circle: you can use the circle of stones for healing yourself or

for healing others. Say you are a therapist, you can get your patient comfortable using whatever way you normally do, and then you can put your stones in a circle around them, so the power of the circle and the powers of these pieces of the Earth and the powers of these winds and directions can all be called upon to help you with whatever you are doing for your patient. You can lay the stones in the directions that will be of benefit to the feelings that they have or the needs that they have. There are many, many different ways to use them, and it's good if we can find our own way of working with them.

LAYING OUT THE STONES

To set out your stones, you lay them in a clockwise direction; that is, in a sunwise direction. When you pick them up, you do the same thing again. You always go sunwise, always lay things out and always pick them up in the same direction.

But if you are looking to the North, then you begin your circle in the North. When you dismantle it, you begin in the East so that you finish picking up in the North before going to the center. (If looking to the South, start your circle there and pick them up beginning in the West—and so on for whatever direction you are relating to.)

THE DIFFERENT USES FOR THE MEDICINE WHEEL

The medicine wheel is the nucleus of an atom; it is the universe, and it is everything in between. It offers a series of circles within circles which correspond to a day, a year, a life and so on. It is a philosophy, a way of thought and a learning tool. It is both a physical solid and pure energy. If you only look at the wheel in its most complex forms, it can be overpowering and confusing; but, for the beginner, the beauty of the medicine wheel is its essential simplicity. Approached simplistically, this naturally shaped structure can be used to explain and understand all the complexities of existence. I remember, as a child, seeing the medicine wheel used in my school books. It was used to show us about the cycle of a cow eating grass: she turned it into milk and her waste product was then used to feed the grass so that it would grow and the cow could feed herself . . . It is in ways like this that we begin to understand life and existence; we begin simply but add the layers slowly to build and develop our knowledge.

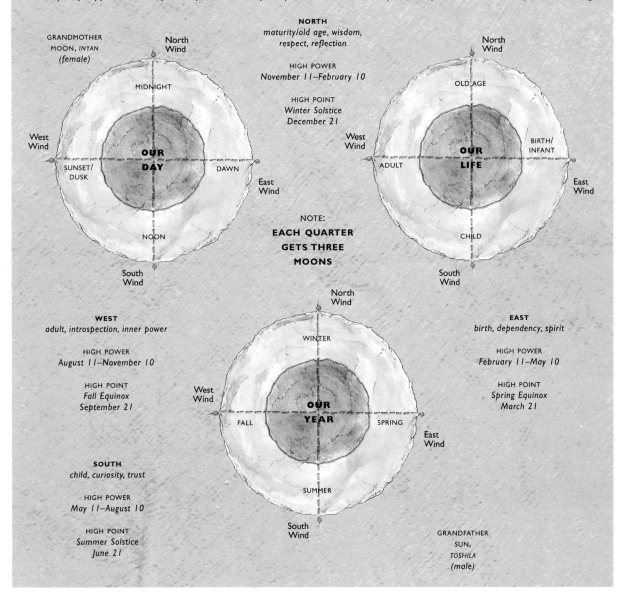

GRANDMOTHER MOON, INYAN (female)

North Wind

MIDNIGHT

West Wind

OUR DAY

SUNSET/ DUSK

DAWN

East Wind

NOON

South Wind

NORTH
maturity/old age, wisdom, respect, reflection

HIGH POWER
November 11–February 10

HIGH POINT
Winter Solstice December 21

NOTE:
EACH QUARTER GETS THREE MOONS

North Wind

OLD AGE

West Wind

OUR LIFE

ADULT

BIRTH/ INFANT

East Wind

CHILD

South Wind

WEST
adult, introspection, inner power

HIGH POWER
August 11–November 10

HIGH POINT
Fall Equinox September 21

SOUTH
child, curiosity, trust

HIGH POWER
May 11–August 10

HIGH POINT
Summer Solstice June 21

North Wind

WINTER

West Wind

FALL

OUR YEAR

SPRING

East Wind

SUMMER

South Wind

EAST
birth, dependency, spirit

HIGH POWER
February 11–May 10

HIGH POINT
Spring Equinox March 21

GRANDFATHER SUN, TOSHILA (male)

ABOVE
*Many people devote their lives to
understanding Mother Earth and her ways. This is
Rolling Thunder, a Cherokee-Shoshone medicine man.*

FOLLOWING A REFLECTIVE WAY

One thing that I need to point out to you is that when you lay your wheel out and when you close your wheel down, you need to follow a reflective way. If, for example, you lay your wheel out in order to use the circle to seek wisdom or understanding, then you begin by laying out with the North and follow to the East, South, and West, going from the earth to the air, to the fire, to the water. When you are laying your stones out and you are looking at a direction, you lay them out going to your chosen direction first, and then your stone, your personal *watai*, the one that you have found and chosen and the one that has chosen you, you set that stone in the direction that you want to look and you move the stone around to what you sense and feel during your examination of the web.

You move it into the directions that you are guided to by your feelings, by your senses, and by your visions. If you are guided to look into the center, or into the Earth, if you are guided to look within yourself, then you move the stone into the section where you originally placed it. You place your stone where you need it to be, but you leave your stone till last to be picked up.

Your *watai* is usually in a bag of its own, because that's the one that always stays in your pocket and that always goes with you wherever you go; you lay it down in your circle with the center stones being the last in the circle to be laid and the first to be picked up. You have chosen the direction on the outer circle of the wheel, and when you have laid your wheel, whichever wind you laid first is the one that you pick up last.

HONORING THE PLACE

Everything is sacred to the Creator. When constructing the Earthweb, I try to find a way of honoring the place where I lay my stones. Traditionally, the medicine man would smudge (cleanse) himself with smoke from the burning sacred herbs of sage, sweetgrass, or cedar, and offer tobacco to the spirit of the place he wished to lay his stones. He would do this by laying a handful of tobacco on the ground and asking permission to work with the energies of this place for a while. The offering was made to give a gift to the energies in return for their cooperation and assistance. By taking time to honor and respect the spirit of a place, it is possible to strengthen your own relationship to the spirits of nature and the energies of the Earth.

Having made my offering, which can be anything (a strand of hair for example), I can lay my stones out. It is not what you give, but how you give it that is important.

FLUID AND CHANGING

Remember that the Earthweb is not fixed. It is like Grandmother Moon—fluid and changing.

ABOVE

Sage is one of the oldest sacred herbs among Native Americans. It goes into kinnick-kinnick *and is burned on its own to cleanse and purify the body.*

Likewise, your stones and crystals may change as the web of your life evolves. The stones that I am using for the winds at the moment may well change over time. This is a perfectly natural thing to happen. I have outlined the stones and crystals that I am using right now in order to help to give you guidelines while you become familiar with the Earthweb. But really, it is best to find your own representative stones, the energies that personify you as a two-legged being and which will be uniquely yours. Your Earthweb will then be directly related to your needs and specifically connected to your own personal journey.

You will need to find four stones that represent the Four Winds, 12 stones to represent the 12 moons, a stone for the Blue Moon, a stone to represent the Creator, a stone to represent the Mother, as well as your personal power stone. This makes 20 stones.

MANY USES, MANY WAYS

When you are asking a question, remember that the answer may not come right away. It may come in a dream, or appear sometime later during your day-to-day activities. Help will come and your question will be answered. Spirit works with each one of us individually. You will find the way that is most comfortable for you. Just remain open and prepared for the answer that is to come.

If you are wanting help or guidance about a work or personal relationship, then you can also put your sun and moon stones down with someone else's stones laid next to them, and you will be able to build up the strands to find your connections and what you may have to learn from and give to each other. The Earthweb can be used to help you in many ways. You can use the teachings contained within it to help you through your day, your year, or your life. Everything has a beginning, a middle, and an end—it all moves in a circle. If you can connect to the particular cycle you are wanting help with, you can see what you may need to do in order to reach a satisfactory result. Call upon one of the Four Winds, for example; or speak with Grandmother Moon.

If you speak with Grandmother Moon, there are certain things you should know. She has four faces, and each face is shown for a different reason. If you are wanting help to let something go, then the best time is during the evening when she is just coming up to her waning time. Offer your prayers, facing the West, and ask for her help. If you are wanting help to bring something new into your life –a loving relationship, for example, –then try talking to her when she is just coming into her new moon phase, while you are facing the direction of the East.

If you are wanting some assistance with increasing your potential, or expanding upon something in your life, do this between the new moon and the full moon while facing South.

ABOVE

*The movement of the running water echoes
that of the ebb and flow of the waters of life,
pulled by the moon on its monthly cycle.*

For wisdom, understanding, and introspection, at times when you need help to clarify what is happening and why, then talk to Grandmother Moon during the dark of the moon, or between the waning moon and the new moon, while facing North.

Now that we have some idea about the questions we may want to ask, we begin with the direction of our chosen wind.

THE DIRECTION OF OUR WINDS

East is the air element and the place of birth and new beginnings; the place of Spirit. I am using amber to represent the East Wind, or the direction of the East, and you may decide to choose a piece of amber to place in this direction, until you find your own crystal to represent the East. Face the direction and lay down your stone. Turning sunwise (clockwise), to the direction of the South Wind, the fire element, you are facing the place of growth, building, and expansion.

I am representing the South Wind by the garnet. You may like to choose a garnet to represent this direction for you. Whether you have a garnet or another chosen stone to represent the South Wind, face the South with it and then lay down your stone. Continue by turning to the West Wind, the place of harvest and giving, and the element of water. I am working with snowflake obsidian at the moment to represent the West Wind.

Taking your chosen crystal, face toward the West and lay down your stone.

Finally, taking the stone that you have chosen to represent the North Wind –and I am using milky quartz as my representative right now–turn to face the North, the direction of wisdom, understanding, and keeping, and lay down your stone. You have turned in a circle and marked the fixed points (the days of Grandfather Sun) on your Earthweb and have connected with the Four Winds. These four chosen stones

BELOW

This is the layout for the Four Winds for my particular stones. I am using green turquoise for the Creator and a river stone for the Mother.

MILKY QUARTZ

THE CREATOR AND MOTHER

RIVER STONE

GREEN TURQUOISE

SNOWFLAKE OBSIDIAN

AMBER

GARNET

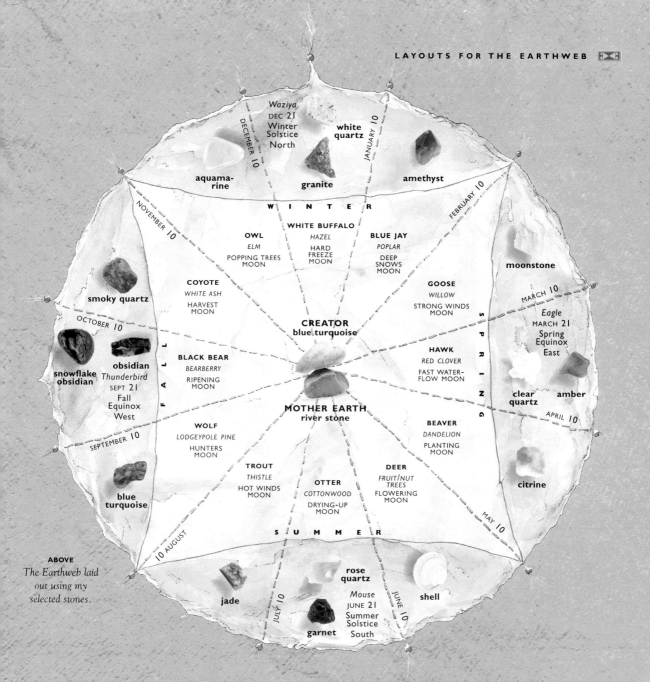

Waziya
DEC 21
Winter
Solstice
North

DECEMBER 10

JANUARY 10

white quartz

aquama-rine

granite

amethyst

NOVEMBER 10

FEBRUARY 10

W I N T E R

moonstone

WHITE BUFFALO
HAZEL
HARD FREEZE MOON

OWL
ELM
POPPING TREES MOON

BLUE JAY
POPLAR
DEEP SNOWS MOON

COYOTE
WHITE ASH
HARVEST MOON

GOOSE
WILLOW
STRONG WINDS MOON

MARCH 10

smoky quartz

Eagle
MARCH 21
Spring Equinox
East

CREATOR
blue turquoise

OCTOBER 10

F
A
L
L

S
P
R
I
N
G

BLACK BEAR
BEARBERRY
RIPENING MOON

HAWK
RED CLOVER
FAST WATER-FLOW MOON

snowflake obsidian

obsidian
Thunderbird
SEPT 21
Fall Equinox
West

clear quartz

amber

APRIL 10

MOTHER EARTH
river stone

WOLF
LODGEYPOLE PINE
HUNTERS MOON

BEAVER
DANDELION
PLANTING MOON

SEPTEMBER 10

citrine

TROUT
THISTLE
HOT WINDS MOON

DEER
FRUIT/NUT TREES
FLOWERING MOON

blue turquoise

OTTER
COTTONWOOD
DRYING-UP MOON

10 AUGUST

MAY 10

S U M M E R

rose quartz

JULY 10

JUNE 10

ABOVE
The Earthweb laid out using my selected stones.

jade

Mouse
JUNE 21
Summer Solstice
South

shell

garnet

---

will represent the winds on your Earthweb. Just remember that whichever wind you are calling upon is the direction that you start with, the direction that you lay down your stone first. When you have completed your time with the stones, you gather them up so that the direction you started with is the last stone you pick up.

THE CREATOR AND MOTHER

Two stones need to be chosen to represent the Creator and the Mother. I use green turquoise to signify the Creator, and because the Mother represents all things of the water, I always use a river stone to portray her energies. The Creator stone needs to be larger than the Mother stone. These two stones should be laid down in the center of your circle, one on top of the other.

FINDING THE MOON AND THE FIRST SEGMENT OF THE WHEEL

So where do we begin finding out about where to put the moons? The closest full moon to the Spring Equinox is where we need to begin. This is the first moon of our year because it is the first strong moon of the year.

The Earthweb doesn't work like traditional astrology does—the dates given here are only a guide—the Earthweb works much more flexibly than that. So we've first of all got to find the first moon of the year. The spring wind will go right through the center, and that's where you look for your full moon. Then you go back to the new moon prior to that full moon and ahead to the new moon following it. This will mark the first segment of the medicine wheel. The four full moons that coincide most closely to the Four Winds will be the most powerful moons of the year.

LOCATION

I make wheels that are sometimes very large and sometimes quite small. Its size is not significant. It can be built inside or outside, upon an altar or upon the ground, depending upon the focus for your wheel, although at some times of the year it is best to set up your wheel outside. Then you can be a

BELOW
The earliest European and American explorers and surveyors of the continental United States were astounded by its vastness and by the scale and majesty of its natural wonders. Thomas Moran's Yellowstone Grand Canyon *captures some of the epic scale.*

part of the web as it is living and growing. The closer you can be to the Earthweb, the better it will be. Each part of the Earth holds unique energies because of the diverse environmental factors that make up each part of her. Her trees, hills, waters, and creatures create differing landscapes that have particular qualities you can draw upon when you are building your Earthweb. Maybe there is a park or some woodland you know of where your stones can be set up, used, and then taken away again, without causing offense to anyone.

CHOICE AND CHANGE

Now we turn to the stones that represent the 13 moons. Like the stones that have been suggested to represent the Four Winds, the rocks that have been suggested to represent the 13 moons are not fixed; they have been provided to help you to get started and to work with the Earthweb until you are confident enough to find your own stones and build your own web. If, at any point, you feel that another stone would be better for your energies for one of the moon's phases, then follow your own intuition and use your own stone instead.

So now I will outline the 13 stones that I am using myself at the moment to represent the moons. Because Grandmother Moon's energies are so linked with the waters of the Earth, you may also decide to use 13 river stones, or perhaps gather some shells or gifts from the sea while you are seeking the stones for your Earthweb. You may even decide to use only river stones or things from the sea to represent the 13 moons. This is entirely up to you.

FAST WATERFLOW MOON—*clear quartz*
PLANTING MOON—*citrine*
FLOWERING MOON—*sea shell*
DRYING-UP MOON—*rose quartz*
HOT WINDS MOON—*jade*
HUNTERS MOON—*blue turquoise*
RIPENING MOON—*obsidian*
HARVEST MOON—*smoky quartz*
POPPING TREES MOON—*aquamarine*
HARD FREEZE MOON—*granite*
DEEP SNOWS MOON—*amethyst*
STRONG WINDS MOON—*moonstone*
THE BLUE MOON—*fool's gold*

LEFT
An ancient public meeting place in Norway. The circle is both natural and practical; the story of the Arthurian round table provides us with an example of the latter— everybody was deliberately given an equal place.

RIGHT
These are my mineral totems, that are used to represent the moons in my Earthweb; you may agree with them or select your own as a result of your personal thoughts, feelings, and visions.

clear quartz   citrine   sea shell   rose quartz   jade   blue turquoise

obsidian   smoky quartz   aquamarine   granite   amethyst   moonstone   fool's gold

PLACING YOUR WATAI

*A*ll that is required to complete the setting up of your Earthweb is your personal power stone or watai, which is held aside and placed upon the web at the point you wish to work with. Whichever direction you need help with is the place to put your personal power stone. Remember that you may require wisdom or understanding, but you may also require help to get it moving, in which case you would set your stone down in the North East (North for wisdom and understanding, and East for new beginnings).

If you have got things started, but need help building it up a little bit, or filling it with energy and focus, then you will need to place your *watai* in the South East (South for expansion and East for new beginnings).

If you are having problems keeping something or someone motivated, you will need to place your *watai* in the South. If things have been going quite well, but you are now not too sure how to complete, then you could lay your *watai* in the South West or the West, depending upon where in your cycle you feel you are. Look at the moon totems and the minerals and plants to give you extra insights into the meanings of Grandmother Moon during the cycles of your day, month, year, or life.

Remember that the North is Grandmother Moon's most powerful time–this is the time of darkness and reflection and going within.

GIVING THANKS

Another important point to let you know about is the giving of thanks. It is important to remember to thank the beings that come to help you, in whatever way you think is good. You could say a prayer, you could offer a gift, you could perform a ceremony. But always remember to thank whatever comes to help you. This way, you will strengthen your connection to the energies, and they will be happy to come to you again because they will feel that you are sincere, they will feel that your heart is in the right place.

THE *WATAI*– YOUR PERSONAL POWER STONE

Each one of us has a *watai*–a piece of Mother Earth that is ours. When searching for your own *watai*, bear in mind what you are looking for. Whether you are looking for the East, or maybe the wisdom of the North, or perhaps a stone to

ABOVE
Medicine bags or pouches are common to most Native Americans and many peoples of the Earth. In them one carries those sacred objects prized by the individual: special stones or watai, animal fetishes, sacred herbs, corn pollen, and so on–anything that has spiritual significance to you. They are rarely opened in front of others except when it is used ceremonially.

represent the eleventh moon. Remember what the eleventh moon is about. Look and see before you go on your search so that you can keep that in mind. But mostly, separate the prejudice or ignorance of Western civilization that this is just a rock. This is not just a rock.

I'd like to share a story about something that I've remembered from when I was younger.

When I went to university and all through high school and out into the everyday world of the modern twentieth century, people talked about "just trees," "just rocks," they are "just cows." They are "just there for us to use." They are there to build a house with, or to climb, or to cut down or break up and make a roadbed out of. But they are more, and I knew this. I knew it as I was being taught, and other people know it in other ways, and knowing it just comes from a feeling in a way, it is that they know things.

When I was at university, in order to get my degree, I had to take a life-science course and your choices in life-science courses were anatomy and physiology, biology, botany, or geology. Geology has got to be better than naming the bones of the body, I thought. I am not good at memorizing things. In anatomy and physiology or botany, you have to memorize a lot of stuff. I didn't think geology would do that to me, but they fooled me. Besides that, it turned out to be a good course, and when I went to pick up the textbook, there was a sense of recognition that not only were we Native Americans different in our way of thinking about this sort of thing, but so were scientists. Because there on the title of the book, it told you its tale,

Our Living Earth, *and that is important to remember. It's not just a rock. It's not just a planet. It's a living being and it has within it—in every piece of it that has separated from the whole, every rock, every grain of sand, every flake of clay—a spirit.*

It is mitakuye oyasin. *It is part of all of our relations. Ho!*

CONNECTING WITH THE ENERGY

The Mother Earth shares her gifts of stones, minerals, and rocks with us as we need them. Our *watai* will arrive when needed and make way as another comes to take its place. The only constant is change. We humans need to move toward what we do not know in order to grow. By using the *watai* on the Earthweb, there will be a connection made to your own relationship with Mother Earth's energies, which will strengthen your connection to the rhythms

LEFT
The medicine wheel, the Earthweb, is absorbed by many Native Americans from childhood, but enlightenment and understanding can come at any age.

and cycles of your life in relation to everything else around you.

Once you have collected the stones, rocks, or crystals that you feel are the right ones for you to be using at the moment, store them in a medicine pouch or small bag, and keep them on your altar or other sacred space until you need to open and use them again. I advise you not to keep your Earthweb set up anywhere, as this will hold it to the time of construction and may keep things from progressing in the appropriate way.

PROTECTING AND CLEANSING

I keep a piece of sage in my medicine pouch, to protect the stones while I am not using them. Sage is one of our sacred herbs that is used in ceremonies. It can be bought from most New Age or Native American stores, but if you can't get hold of any sage (not the dried sage you can buy that comes in herb jars, but the wild kind you go out and gather using prayers and giving offerings of thanks), you can use some juniper or bay laurel. This would need to be gathered in the same sacred way. Any of these herbs will help to keep your stones clean while they are resting in your pouches.

When I need to cleanse my stones and crystals, personally I use a shell as a container. I use

self-igniting charcoal as fuel because it tends to be readily available and not difficult to use, even indoors, as long as you are careful not to leave your warm shell on something that will burn. I've done that a couple of times. I've scorched some straw mats in my day and burned a few holes in the carpet with the bottom of a hot shell. So be very careful.

Whether you cleanse them with something of the air, by smudging, or with water or with salt, do this in the best way that is suitable for yourself; but to give you some ideas to start with, you can cleanse your crystals and stones using the powers of the Four Winds, the powers of air, fire, water, and earth. You can place your crystals of the East toward the East Wind and let it blow upon them, or pass them through the smoke of some sacred cleansing herbs. You can pass your South Wind crystals through the fire of a candle flame. You can rinse your crystals for the West in the ocean, clear rivers, or streams. You can bury your earth stones of the North within the earth. Give them as much time as you can to rebalance themselves before you collect them for your use again. This could be as much as a day or a night. Again, let the stones tell you what they need, and listen to what your intuition tells you. Your intuition, you see, is the voice that spirit uses to talk with you.

Salt water is a powerful cleanser. If you cannot get to a source of the natural elements too

easily, then you can fill a container with spring water (available from most general stores in bottles), adding about a tablespoonful of salt to it and mixing it around a little bit. Put your stones that need cleansing in the water and leave them to stand for a good few hours. Rinse them off with spring water, hold them, and rededicate them to their purpose and position upon your Earthweb. You can then put them aside until you are ready to open up the bag and use them again. I tend to clean my stones about once every two months, or when they don't look or feel so bright or vibrant. You are the best one to judge when you think your stones need a cleansing.

OFFERING THANKS

The way to offer prayers to the spirits of nature is from the heart. Feel your way to their energy, communicate with them, tell them what you are wanting to use them for, and ask them if they would mind giving a part of themselves to you for use with your Earthweb.

When I am taking anything from Mother Earth, I always remember to make some kind of offering. When I pick or cut what I need, I leave something of myself as a thank-you. This could be anything, as long as it means something. It doesn't have to cost much, but it should really mean something.—*Mitakuye oyasin, a ho!*

BELOW
The Great Smoky Mountains of North Carolina are home to the Cherokee. The characteristic hazes are caused by vapor from the heavy vegetation. The Cherokee know of many mountain places associated with the thunder-beings.

Year	Moon	Fast Water-Flow	Planting	Flowering	Drying-up	Hot Winds	Hunter's	Ripening	Harvest	Popping Trees	Hard Freeze	Deep Snows
1930–31	FULL	14/3	13/4	12/5	11/6							
	NEW	30/3	28/4	28/5	26/6	25/7	24/8	22/9	21/10	20/11	20/12	18/1
	FULL				10/7	9/8	8/9	7/10	6/11	6/12	4/1	3/2
1931–32	NEW	19/3	18/4	17/5	16/6	15/7	13/8	12/9	11/10			
	FULL	2/4	2/5	31/5	30/6	29/7	28/8	26/9	26/10	25/11	24/12	23/1
	NEW								9/11	9/12	7/1	6/2
1932–33	FULL	22/3	20/4	20/5	18/6	17/7	16/8	17/9	14/10	13/11	13/12	11/1
	NEW	6/4	5/5	4/6	3/7	2/8	31/8	30/9	29/10	28/11	27/12	25/1
	FULL											10/2
1933–34	NEW	26/3	24/4	24/5	23/6	22/7	21/8	19/9	19/10	17/11	17/12	15/1
	FULL	10/4	9/5	8/6	7/7	5/8	4/9	3/10	2/11	2/12	31/12	30/1
1934–35	NEW	15/3	13/4	13/5	12/6	11/7						
	FULL	31/3	29/4	28/5	27/6	26/7	24/8	23/9	22/10	21/11	20/12	19/1
	NEW						10/8	9/9	8/10	7/11	6/12	5/1	3/2
1935–36	FULL	20/3	21/4	18/5	16/6	16/7	14/8	12/9	12/10			
	NEW	3/4	2/5	1/6	30/6	30/7	29/8	27/9	27/10	26/11	25/12	24/1
	FULL								10/11	10/12	8/1	7/2
1936–37	NEW	23/3	21/4	20/5	19/6	18/7	17/8	15/9	15/10	14/11	13/12	12/1
	FULL	6/4	6/5	5/6	4/7	3/8	1/9	30/9	30/10	28/11	28/12	26/1
1937–38	NEW	12/3	11/4									
	FULL	26/3	25/4	25/5	23/6	23/7	22/8	20/9	19/10	18/11	17/12	16/1
	NEW		10/5	8/6	8/7	6/8	4/9	4/10	3/11	2/12	1/1	31/1
1938–39	FULL	16/3	14/4	14/5	12/6	12/7	11/8					
	NEW	31/3	30/4	29/5	27/6	27/7	25/8	23/9	23/10	22/11	21/12	20/7
	FULL						9/9	9/10	7/11	7/12	5/1	4/2
1939–40	NEW	21/3	19/4	19/5	17/6	16/7	15/8	13/9	12/10	11/11		
	FULL	4/4	3/5	2/6	1/7	31/7	29/8	28/9	28/10	26/11	26/12	24/1
	NEW									10/12	9/1	8/2
1940–41	FULL	23/3	22/4	21/5	19/6	19/7	17/8	16/9	16/10	15/11	14/12	13/1
	NEW	7/4	7/5	6/6	5/7	3/8	2/9	1/10	30/10	19/11	28/12	27/1

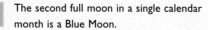

The second full moon in a single calendar month is a Blue Moon.

Year	Moon	Fast Water-Flow	Planting	Flowering	Drying-Up	Hot Winds	Hunter's	Ripening	Harvest	Popping Trees	Hard Freeze	Deep Snows	Strong Winds
–42	FULL	13/3	11/44	11/5									
	NEW	27/3	26/4	26/5	24/6	24/7	22/8	21/9	20/10	19/11	18/12	16/1	15/2
	FULL			9/6	8/7	7/8	5/9	5/10	4/11	3/12	2/1	1/2	3/3
2–43	NEW	16/3	15/4	15/5	13/6	13/7	12/8						
	FULL	1/4	30/4	30/5	28/6	27/7	26/8	24/9	24/10	22/11	22/12	21/1	20/2
	NEW						10/9	10/10	8/11	8/12	6/1	4/2	6/3
3–44	FULL	21/3	20/4	19/5	18/6	17/7	15/8	14/9	13/10	12/11	11/12		
	NEW	4/4	4/5	2/6	2/7	1/8	30/8	29/9	29/10	27/11	27/12	25/1	24/2
	FULL										10/1	9/2	10/3
4–45	NEW	24/3	22/4	22/5	10/6	10/7	18/8	17/9	17/10	15/11	15/12	14/1	12/2
	FULL	8/4	8/5	6/6	6/7	4/8	2/9	2/10	31/10	30/11	29/12	28/1	27/2
5–46	NEW	14/3	12/4	11/5									
	FULL	28/3	27/4	27/5	25/6	25/7	23/8	21/9	21/10	19/11	19/12	17/1	16/2
	NEW			10/6	9/7	8/8	6/9	6/10	4/11	4/12	3/1	2/2	3/3
6–47	FULL	17/3	16/4	16/5	14/6	14/7	12/8	11/9					
	NEW	2/4	1/5	30/5	29/6	28/7	26/8	25/9	25/10	23/11	23/12	22/1	21/2
	FULL							10/10	9/11	8/12	7/1	5/2	7/3
7–48	NEW	22/3	21/4	20/5	18/6	18/7	16/8	14/9	14/10	12/11	12/12	11/1	
	FULL	5/4	5/5	3/6	3/7	2/8	31/8	30/9	29/10	28/11	27/12	26/1	24/2
	NEW											10/2	10/3
8–49	FULL	24/3	23/4	23/5	21/6	21/7	19/8	18/9	18/10	16/11	16/12	14/1	13/2
	NEW	9/4	9/5	7/6	6/77	5/8	3/9	2/10	1/11	30/11	30/12	29/1	27/2
9–50	FULL	14/3	13/4	12/5									
	NEW	29/3	28/4	27/5	26/6	25/7	24/8	22/9	21/10	20/11	19/12	18/1	16/2
	FULL			10/6	10/7	8/8	7/9	7/10	5/11	5/12	4/1	2/2	4/3
0–51	NEW	18/3	17/4	17/5	15/6	15/7	13/8	12/9	11/10				
	FULL	2/4	2/5	31/5	29/6	29/7	27/8	26/9	25/10	24/11	24/12	23/1	21/2
	NEW									9/11	9/12	7/1	6/2	7/3
1–52	NEW	23/3	23/4	21/5	19/6	18/7	17/8	15/9	15/10	13/11	13/12	12/1	11/2
	FULL	5/4	6/5	4/6	4/7	2/8	1/9	30/8	1/10	29/11	28/12	26/1	25/2

Year	Moon	Fast Water-Flow	Planting	Flowering	Drying-Up	Hot Winds	Hunter's	Ripening	Harvest	Popping Trees	Hard Freeze	Deep Snows	Ste…
1952-53	FULL	11/3											
	NEW	25/3	24/4	23/5	22/6	21/7	20/8	19/9	18/10	17/11	17/12	15/2	
	FULL	10/4	9/5	8/6	7/7	5/8	4/9	3/10	1/11	1/12	31/12	29/1	
1953-54	NEW	15/3	13/4	13/5	11/6	11/7							
	FULL	30/3	29/4	28/5	27/6	26/7	24/8	23/9	22/10	20/11	20/12	19/1	
	NEW					9/8	8/9	8/10	6/11	6/12	5/1	3/2	
1954-55	FULL	19/3	18/4	17/5	16/6	16/7	14/8	12/9	12/10				
	NEW	3/4	3/5	1/6	30/6	29/7	26/8	27/9	26/10	26/11	25/12	24/1	
	FULL								10/11	10/12	8/1	7/2	
1955-56	NEW	24/3	22/4	21/5	20/6	19/7	17/8	16/9	15/10	14/11	14/12	13/1	
	FULL	7/4	6/5	5/6	5/7	3/8	2/9	1/10	31/10	29/11	29/12	27/1	
1956-57	NEW	12/3	11/4										
	FULL	26/3	25/4	24/5	23/6	22/7	21/8	20/9	19/10	18/11	17/12	16/1	
	NEW		10/5	8/6	8/7	6/8	4/9	4/10	2/11	2/12	1/1	30/1	
1957-58	FULL	16/3	14/4	13/5	12/6	11/7							
	NEW	31/3	29/4	29/5	27/6	27/7	25/8	23/9	23/10	21/11	21/12	19/1	
	FULL					10/8	9/9	8/10	7/11	7/12	5/1	4/2	
1958-59	NEW	20/3	19/4	18/5	17/6	16/7	15/8	13/9	12/10	11/11			
	FULL	4/4	3/5	1/6	1/7	30/7	29/8	27/9	27/10	26/11	26/12	24/1	
	NEW									10/12	9/1	7/2	
1959-60	FULL	14/3	23/4	22/5	20/6	20/7	18/8	17/9	15/10	15/11	15/12	13/1	
	NEW	8/4	7/5	6/6	6/7	4/8	3/9	2/10	31/10	30/11	29/12	28/1	
1960-61	FULL	13/3	11/4	11/5									
	NEW	27/3	25/4	25/5									
	FULL			9/6	8/7	7/8	5/9	4/10	3/11	3/12	1/1	31/1	
1961-62	NEW	15/3	15/4	14/5	13/6	12/7	11/8						
	FULL	30/3	30/4	30/5	28/6	27/7	26/8	24/9	23/10	22/11	22/12	20/1	
	NEW						10/9	9/10	8/11	7/12	6/1	5/2	

	MOON	FAST WATER-FLOW	PLANTING	FLOWERING	DRYING-UP	HOT WINDS	HUNTER'S	RIPENING	HARVEST	POPPING TREES	HARD FREEZE	DEEP SNOWS	STRONG WINDS
–63	FULL	21/3	20/4	19/5	18/6	17/7	15/8	14/9	13/10	11/11	11/12		
	NEW	4/4	4/5	3/6	1/7	31/7	30/8	28/9	28/10	27/11	26/12	25/1	24/2
	FULL										9/1	8/2	10/3
–64	NEW	25/3	23/4	23/5	21/6	20/7	19/8	17/9	17/10	16/11	16/12	14/1	13/2
	FULL	9/4	8/5	7/6	6/7	5/8	3/9	3/10	1/11	30/11	30/12	18/1	27/2
–65	NEW	14/3	12/4	11/5									
	FULL	28/3	26/4	26/5	25/6	24/7	23/8	21/9	21/10	19/11	19/12	17/1	16/2
	NEW			10/6	9/7	7/8	6/9	5/10	4/11	4/12	2/1	1/2	3/3
–66	FULL	17/3	15/4	15/5	14/6	13/7	12/8						
	NEW	2/4	1/5	30/5	29/6	28/7	26/8	25/9	24/10	23/11	22/12	21/1	20/2
	FULL						10/9	10/10	9/11	8/12	7/1	5/2	7/3
–67	NEW	22/3	20/4	20/5	18/6	18/7	16/8	14/9	14/10	12/11	12/12		
	FULL	5/4	4/5	3/6	2/7	1/8	31/8	29/9	29/10	28/11	27/12	26/1	27/2
	NEW										10/1	9/2	11/3
–69	FULL	13/3	12/4										
	NEW	27/3	27/4	27/5	25/6	25/7	23/8	22/9	21/10	20/11	19/12	18/1	16/2
	FULL		10/5	10/6	10/7	8/8	6/9	6/10	5/11	4/12	3/1	2/2	4/3
–70	NEW	18/3	16/4	16/5	14/6	14/7	13/8	11/9	11/10				
	FULL	2/4	2/5	31/5	29/6	29/7	27/8	25/9	25/10	23/11	23/12	22/1	21/2
	NEW									9/11	9/12	7/1	6/2	7/3
–71	FULL	23/3	21/4	21/5	19/6	18/7	17/8	15/9	14/10	13/11	12/12	11/1		
	NEW	6/4	5/5	4/6	3/7	2/8	31/8	30/9	30/10	28/11	28/12	26/1	25/2
	FULL											10/2		
–72	FULL	12/3											
	NEW	26/3	24/4	24/5	22/6	22/7	20/8	19/9	19/10	18/11	17/12	16/1	15/2
	FULL	10/4	10/5	9/6	8/7	6/8	5/9	4/10	2/11	2/12	31/12	30/1	29/2
–73	NEW	13/3	13/4	13/5	11/6								
	FULL	29/3	28/4	28/5	26/6	26/7	24/8	23/9	22/10	20/11	20/12	18/1	17/2
	NEW					10/7	9/8	7/9	7/10	6/11	5/12	4/1	3/2	5/3

Year	Moon	Fast Water-Flow	Planting	Flowering	Drying-Up	Hot Winds	Hunter's	Ripening	Harvest	Popping Trees	Hard Freeze	Deep Snows	S…
1973–74	Full	16/3	17/4	17/5	15/6	15/7	14/8	12/9	12/10				
	New	3/4	2/5	1/6	30/6	29/7	28/8	26/9	26/10	24/11	24/12	23/1	
	Full								10/11	10/12	8/1	6/2	
1974–75	New	23/3	22/4	21/5	20/6	19/7	17/8	16/9	15/10	14/11	13/12	12/1	
	Full	6/4	6/5	4/6	4/7	3/8	1/9	1/10	31/10	29/11	29/12	27/1	
1975–76	New	12/3	11/4	11/5									
	Full	27/3	25/4	25/5	23/6	23/7	21/8	20/9	20/10	18/11	18/12	17/1	
	New			9/6	9/7	7/8	5/9	5/10	3/11	3/12	1/1	31/1	
1976–77	Full	16/3	14/4	13/5	12/6	11/7							
	New	30/3	29/4	29/5	27/6	27/7	25/8	23/9	23/10	21/11	21/12	19/1	
	Full					9/8	8/9	8/10	6/11	6/12	5/1	4/2	
1977–78	New	19/3	18/4	18/5	16/6	16/7	14/8	13/9	12/10	11/11			
	Full	4/4	3/5	1/6	1/7	30/7	28/8	27/9	26/10	25/11	25/12	24/1	
	New									10/12	9/1	7/2	
1978–79	Full	24/3	23/4	22/5	20/6	20/7	18/8	16/9	16/10	14/11	14/12	13/1	
	New	7/4	7/5	5/6	5/7	4/8	2/9	2/10	31/10	30/11	29/12	28/1	
1979–80	Full	13/3	12/4	12/5									
	New	28/3	26/4	26/5	24/6	24/7	22/8	21/9	21/10	19/11	19/12	17/1	
	Full			10/6	9/7	8/8	6/9	5/10	4/11	3/12	2/1	1/2	
1980–81	New	16/3	15/4	14/5	12/6	12/7							
	Full	31/3	30/4	29/5	28/6	27/7	26/8	24/9	23/10	22/11	21/12	20/1	
	New					10/8	9/9	9/10	7/11	7/12	6/1	4/2	
1981–82	Full	20/3	19/4	19/5	17/6	17/7	15/8	14/9	13/10	11/11	11/12		
	New	4/4	4/5	2/6	1/7	31/7	29/8	28/9	27/10	26/11	26/12	25/1	
	Full										9/1	8/2	
1982–83	New	25/3	23/4	23/5	21/6	20/7	19/8	17/9	17/10	15/11	15/12	14/1	
	Full	8/4	8/5	6/6	6/7	4/8	3/9	3/10	1/11	1/12	31/12	29/1	
1983–84	New	14/3	13/4	12/5	11/6								
	Full	28/3	27/4	26/5	25/6	24/7	23/8	22/9	21/10	20/11	20/12	18/1	
	New				10/7	8/8	7/9	6/10	4/11	4/12	3/1	1/2	

R	MOON	FAST WATER-FLOW	PLANTING	FLOWERING	DRYING-UP	HOT WINDS	HUNTER'S	RIPENING	HARVEST	POPPING TREES	HARD FREEZE	DEEP SNOWS	STRONG WINDS
4–85	FULL	17/3	15/4	15/5	13/6	13/7	11/8						
	NEW	1/4	1/5	30/5	29/6	28/7	26/8	25/9	24/10	22/11	22/12	21/1	19/2
	FULL						10/9	9/10	8/11	8/12	7/1	5/2	7/3
5–86	NEW	21/3	20/4	19/5	18/6	17/7	16/8	14/9	14/10	12/11	12/12		
	FULL	5/4	4/5	3/6	2/7	31/7	30/8	29/9	28/10	27/11	27/12	26/1	24/2
	NEW										10/1	9/2	10/3
6–87	FULL	26/3	24/4	23/5	22/6	21/7	19/8	18/9	17/10	16/11	16/12	15/1	13/2
	NEW	9/4	8/5	7/6	7/7	5/8	4/9	3/10	2/11	1/12	31/12	29/1	28/2
7–88	FULL	15/3	14/4	13/5	11/6	11/7							
	NEW	29/3	28/4	27/5	26/6	25/7	24/8	23/9	22/10	21/11	20/12	19/1	17/2
	FULL					9/8	7/9	7/10	5/11	5/12	4/1	2/2	3/3
8–89	NEW	18/3	16/4	15/5	14/6	13/7	12/8	11/9					
	FULL	2/4	1/5	31/5	29/6	29/7	27/8	25/9	25/10	23/11	23/12	21/1	20/2
	NEW								10/10	9/11	9/12	7/1	6/2	7/3
9–90	FULL	22/3	21/4	20/5	19/6	18/7	17/8	15/9	14/10	13/11	12/12	11/1	
	NEW	6/4	5/5	3/6	3/7	1/8	31/8	29/9	29/10	28/11	28/12	26/1	25/2
	FULL											9/2	11/3
0–91	NEW	26/3	25/4	24/5	22/6	22/7	20/8	19/9	18/10	17/11	17/12	15/1	14/2
	FULL	10/4	9/5	8/6	8/7	6/8	5/9	4/10	2/11	2/12	31/12	30/1	28/2
1–92	NEW	16/3	14/4	14/5	12/6	11/7							
	FULL	30/3	28/4	28/5	27/6	26/7	25/8	23/9	23/10	21/11	21/12	19/1	18/2
	NEW						10/8	8/9	7/10	6/11	6/12	4/1	3/2	4/3
2–93	FULL	18/3	17/4	16/5	15/6	14/7	13/8	12/9	11/10				
	NEW	3/4	2/5	1/6	30/6	29/7	28/8	26/9	25/10	24/11	24/12	22/1	21/2
	FULL								10/11	9/12	8/1	6/2	8/3
3–94	NEW	23/3	21/4	21/5	20/6	19/7	17/8	16/9	15/10	13/11	13/12	11/1	
	FULL	6/4	6/5	4/6	3/7	2/8	1/9	30/9	30/10	29/11	28/12	27/1	26/2
	NEW												10/2	
4–95	NEW	12/3	11/4										
	FULL	27/3	25/4	25/5	23/6	22/7	21/8	19/9	19/10	18/11	18/12	16/1	15/2
	NEW		10/5	9/6	8/7	7/8	5/9	5/10	3/11	2/12	1/1	30/1	1/3

Year	Moon	Fast Water-Flow	Planting	Flowering	Drying-Up	Hot Winds	Hunter's	Ripening	Harvest	Popping Trees	Hard Freeze	Deep Snows	Str... W...
1995–96	FULL	17/3	15/4	14/5	13/6	12/7							
	NEW	31/3	29/4	29/5	28/6	27/7	26/8	24/9	24/10	22/11	22/12	20/1	
	FULL					10/8	9/9	8/10	7/11	7/12	5/1	4/2	
1996–97	NEW	19/3	17/4	17/5	16/6	15/7	14/8	12/9	12/10	11/11			
	FULL	4/4	3/5	1/6	1/7	30/7	28/8	27/9	26/10	25/11	24/12	23/1	
	NEW									10/12	9/1	7/2	
1997–98	FULL	16/3	22/4	22/5	20/6	20/7	18/8	16/9	16/10	14/11	14/12	12/1	
	NEW	7/4	6/5	5/6	4/7	3/8	1/9	1/10	31/10	30/11	29/12	28/1	
1998–99	FULL	13/3	11/4	11/5									
	NEW	28/3	26/4	25/5	24/6	23/7	22/8	20/9	20/10	19/11	18/12	17/1	
	FULL			10/6	9/7	8/8	6/9	5/10	4/11	3/12	2/1	31/1	
1999–2000	NEW	17/3	16/4	15/5	13/6	13/7	11/8						
	FULL	31/3	30/4	30/5	28/6	28/7	26/8	25/9	24/10	23/11	22/12	21/1	
	NEW							9/9	9/10	8/11	7/12	6/1	5/2
2000–01	FULL	20/3	18/4	18/5	16/6	16/7	15/8	13/9	13/10	11/11	11/12		
	NEW	4/4	4/5	2/6	1/7	31/7	29/8	27/9	27/10	25/11	25/12	24/1	
	FULL										9/1	8/2	
2001–02	NEW	25/3	23/4	23/5	21/6	20/7	19/8	16/9	15/10	14/11	13/12	13/1	
	FULL	8/4	7/5	6/6	5/7	4/8	2/9	1/10	30/10	30/11	28/12	29/1	
2002–03	NEW	14/3	12/4	12/5									
	FULL	28/3	27/4	26/5	24/6	24/7	22/8	21/9	21/10	20/11	19/12	18/1	
	NEW			10/6	10/7	8/8	7/9	6/10	4/11	4/12	2/1	1/2	
2003–04	FULL	18/3	16/4	16/5	14/6	13/7	12/8						
	NEW	1/4	1/5	31/5	29/6	29/7	27/8	26/9	25/10	23/11	23/12	21/1	
	FULL						10/9	10/10	9/11	8/12	7/1	6/2	
2004–05	NEW	20/3	19/4	19/5	17/6	17/7	16/8	14/9	14/10	12/11	12/12		
	FULL	5/4	4/5	3/6	2/7	31/7	30/8	28/9	28/10	26/11	26/12	25/1	
	NEW										10/1	8/2	
2005–06	FULL	25/3	24/4	23/5	22/6	21/7	19/8	18/9	17/10	16/11	15/12	14/1	
	NEW	8/4	8/5	6/6	6/7	5/8	3/9	3/10	2/11	1/12	31/12	29/1	

AR	MOON	FAST WATER-FLOW	PLANTING	FLOWERING	DRYING-UP	HOT WINDS	HUNTER'S	RIPENING	HARVEST	POPPING TREES	HARD FREEZE	DEEP SNOWS	STRONG WINDS
6–07	FULL	14/3	13/4	13/5	11/6	11/7							
	NEW	29/3	27/4	27/5	25/6	25/7	23/8	22/9	22/10	20/11	20/12	19/1	17/2
	FULL					9/8	7/9	7/10	5/11	5/12	3/1	2/2	3/3
7–08	NEW	19/3	17/4	16/5	15/6	14/7	12/8	11/9	11/10				
	FULL	2/4	2/5	1/6	30/6	30/7	28/8	26/9	26/10	24/11	24/12	22/1	21/2
	NEW								9/11	9/12	8/1	7/2	7/3
8–09	FULL	21/3	20/4	20/5	18/6	18/7	16/8	15/9	14/10	13/11	12/12	11/1	
	NEW	6/4	5/5	3/6	3/7	1/8	30/8	29/9	28/10	27/11	27/12	26/1	25/2
	FULL											9/2	
9–10	FULL	11/3											
	NEW	26/3	25/4	24/5	22/6	22/7	20/8	18/9	18/10	16/11	16/12	15/1	14/2
	FULL	9/4	9/5	7/6	7/7	6/8	4/9	4/10	2/11	2/12	31/12	30/1	28/2

BLUE MOONS

Blue moons really do exist. They occur when there is an abundance of certain particles in the Earth's atmosphere. The light from the moon, although it appears white, is made up from all the colors of the spectrum. These particles filter out and scatter the colors at one end of the spectrum (the reds and yellows), whilst intensifying the colors at the other end of the spectrum (the blues and greens). This gives the moon a blue or blue-green look, especially if it is viewed when low on the horizon.

Dust from forest fires can turn the moon blue and when volcanoes erupt the dust produced can have the same effect. Blue moons resulting from some powerful change in the atmosphere only come occasionally.

NO GOOD OR BAD LUCK, ONLY POWER

If there are two full moons in one calendar month, the second full moon is called a Blue Moon. People tend to equate it with bad luck, but this comes from a lack of understanding. There is no good or bad luck in creation, only power. It is how we use that power that turns things good or bad. These Blue Moons occur about once every two and a half years. They occur most frequently in months with 31 days in them and only rarely in months with 30 days.

In some of the moon months, when you look at the phases of the actual moon during that month, you will find that there are two full moons. The second full moon is the Blue Moon and this doubles the power of that month's influence. It means that the person born under the Blue Moon will have a much stronger power to utilize in their lives. That power will also have the potential to weaken them twice as much as it would others. For instance, someone born under a Blue Moon in the East will have twice the enlightenment, but they will also have twice the trouble bringing ideas to maturity. The Blue Moon is a two-edged sword.

INDEX

A

amber 41, 114
amethyst 94, 104, 117
animal totems 32–7
aquamarine 87, 117
aura 103
azurite 104

B

bay laurel 120
bear 30–1, 76
bearberry 79
beaver 56, 57, 59
black bear 76
black quartz 82
blue jay 92
Blue Moon 46, 100–1, 117, 129
blue turquoise 75, 117

C

citrine 59, 117
cleansing 120–1
clear quartz 54, 117
cottonwood tree 64, 66
coyote 80–1
Creator 115
curiosity 9

D

dandelion 59
darkness 12
deep blue 79
Deep Snows Moon 50, 92–5, 117
deer 62
dependency 7
dove grey 99
dreamcatchers 33–4, 36
Drying-up Moon 49, 64–7, 117

E

eagle 5, 7
East 4–8, 39–40, 46, 47-9,
    52–3, 114
eleventh moon 119
elm 84
enlightenment 4, 5, 17
equinoxes 39, 42, 46, 47, 50,
    51, 116

F

Fall 41–2
    Equinox 42
    Moons 49–50, 104
Fast Waterflow Moon 48, 52–4, 117
Father Sun 51
Flowering Moon 49, 60–3, 117
fool's gold 101, 117
fossils 104
Four Winds 39–43, 114–15, 120
fruit trees 62–3
full moons 46, 48

G

garnet 41, 114
goose 96–7
Grandfather Sun 39, 40–1, 43, 64
Grandmother Moon 39, 41, 43,
    46–7, 51, 112, 114, 118
granite 91, 117
green 71
green turquoise 115

H

Hard Freeze Moon 50, 88–91, 117
Harvest Moon 49, 50, 80–3, 117
hawk 54
hazel tree 88
healing circle 108
Heyoka wheel 102–5
Hot Winds Moon 49, 68–70, 117
Hunters Moon 49, 72–5, 117

I

indigo 87
innocence 10–11
Inyan 21–2, 24
iron pyrites 101

J

Jack Frost *see Waziya*
jade 71, 117
juniper 120

K

kinnick-kinnick 26, 54, 79

L

light 4–5
lodge pole pine 73

M

milky quartz 43, 114
mitakuye oyasin 3, 103
Moons
    Blue 46, 100–1, 117, 129
    cycles 44–51
    Deep Snows 50, 92–5, 117
    Drying-up 49, 64–7, 117
    eleventh 119
    Fall 49–50, 104
    Fast Waterflow 48, 52–4, 117
    Flowering 49, 60–3, 117
    full 46, 48
    Grandmother 39, 41, 43, 46–7,
        51, 112, 114, 118
    Hard Freeze 50, 88–91, 117
    Harvest 49, 50, 80–3, 117
    Hot Winds 49, 68–70, 117
    Hunters 49, 72–5, 117
    Planting 48–9, 56–9, 117
    Popping Trees 50, 84–7, 117
    Ripening 49–50, 76–9, 117
    Spring 47–9, 104

Strong Winds 48, 96–99, 117
  Summer 49, 104
  Winter 50–1, 104
moonstone 99, 117
Mother 115
Mother Earth 119, 121
mouse 9–10, 41, 62

N

North 16–19, 42–3, 50–1, 114
nut trees 62–3

O

obsidian 79, 117
offering thanks 111, 118, 121
orange 63
otter 64, 66
owl 84–5, 87

P

patience 36–7
petrified wood 104
plant people 26–31
Planting Moon 48–9, 56–9, 117
poplar tree 94
Popping Trees Moon 50, 84–7, 117
protection 120
purple 82

Q

quartz 43, 54, 66, 82, 114, 117

R

record-keeper crystals 104
red 11, 66
red clover 54
red hawk 13–15
red willow 97
Ripening Moon 49–50, 76–79, 117
river stones 115, 117
rose quartz 66, 117
rowan 81

S

saffron 59
sage 26, 103, 120
salt water 120–1
sea shell 63, 117
smoky quartz 82, 117
smudging 120
snake 100–1
snowflake obsidian 42, 114
solstices 40, 41, 43, 46, 50, 51, 64
South 9–11, 40–1, 49, 114
spider 35–7
Spring 39–40
  Equinox 39, 46, 47, 50, 116
  moons 47–9, 104
Stone people 21–5, 104
stones 103–5, 112, 120–1
Strong Winds Moon 48,
  96–9, 117
Summer 40–1
  Moons 49, 104
  Solstice 40, 41, 46, 51, 64
sweetgrass 26, 101, 103

T

tenacity 35–6
thistle 69–70
thunder-beings 14–15, 42
thunderbird 13–14, 41–2
totems 32–7, 103–5
trout 69
trust 10–11

V

violet 94

W

watai 22–5, 111, 118–21
water reed 101
Waziya 16, 42, 89, 91
West 12–15, 41–2, 49–50, 114
white 91
white ash 81
white buffalo 89
willow 97, 99
Winter 42–3
  Moons 50–1, 104
  Solstice 43, 50, 51
wisdom 16–19, 43
wolf 73

Y

yellow 54
yew 30–1

Z

zodiac 46

ACKNOWLEDGMENTS

Bridgeman Art Library: pp. viiiB, 10T, 12B, 18TL (Christie's Images); 43BR (US Capitol Collection, Washington, DC); 52BR; 63; 83 (Brooklyn Museum of Art, New York); 98 (Rijksmuseum Kroller-Muller, Otterlo); 101TR (Museum of the North American Indian, New York); 116 (Reynolds Museum, Winston Salem)

Cameron Collection: pp. 8, 36, 81

Fine Art Photographic: pp. 45, 73

Fortean Picture Library: pp. 1B (Klaus Aarsleff); 110 (Dr Elmar R Gruber)

The Hutchison Library: pp. 30TR, 31B

Images Colour Library: pp. xTR (National Geographic), 2T, 3 (National Geographic), 46BR, 89B

The Stock Market: pp. xi, 2B, 11T, 13T, 14TL, 16B, 21C, 22, 24TL, 29, 33TL, 34B, 37, 40, 42TL, 48, 53, 55, 58, 61, 65, 69B, 70, 74, 78, 82, 86, 95, 99, 102B, 107, 113, 121

Werner Forman Archive: pp. viiiTL Field Museum of Natural History, Chicago; 5T Plains Indian Museum, Buffalo Bill Historical Center, Cody, Wyoming: 5B National Museum of Man, Ottowa; 7B National Museum of Man, Ottawa; 15T Field Museum of Natural History, Chicago; 24BR L Larom Coll., Plains Indian Museum, BBHC, Cody, Wyoming; 33TR A Sponr Coll., Plains Indian Museum, BBHC, Cody, Wyoming; 43TL Maxwell Museum of Anthropology, Albuquerque; 46TL

Glenbow Museum, Calgary, Alberta; 49 British Museum; 50 Smithsonian Institution; 51 Provincial Museum, Victoria, British Colombia, Museum no.1564; 59B National Museum of Man, Ottoawa, Ontario; 64L The American Museum of NaturalHistory; 66B Field Museum of Natural History, Chicago; 71C Mr & Mrs John A Putnam; 75TL National Museum of Man, Ottawa, Ontario; 77; 79TR Plains Indian Museum, Buffalo Bill Historical Center, Cody, Wyoming; 86 Provincial Museum, Victoria, British Colpmbia; 89T Glenbow Museum, Calgary, Alberta; 100L R L Anderson Coll., Plains Indian Museum, BBHC, Cody, Wyoming